Small Business Management

A Road Map for Survival During Crisis

Andreas Karaoulanis

BUSINESS EXPERT PRESS

Small Business Management: A Road Map for Survival During Crisis
Copyright © Business Expert Press, LLC, 2020.

First published in 2020 by
Business Expert Press, LLC
222 East 46th Street, New York, NY 10017
www.businessexpertpress.com

ISBN-13: 978-1-95152-734-1 (paperback)
ISBN-13: 978-1-95152-735-8 (e-book)

Business Expert Press Entrepreneurship and Small Business Management Collection

Collection ISSN: 1946-5653 (print)
Collection ISSN: 1946-5661 (electronic)

Cover image licensed by Ingram Image, StockPhotoSecrets.com
Cover and interior design by S4Carlisle Publishing Services Private Ltd., Chennai, India

First edition: 2020

10 9 8 7 6 5 4 3 2 1

Printed in the United States of America.

Abstract

This book gives us a holistic description of all paragons involved in small business operations during crisis years and suggests the necessary steps that need to be taken to help them overcome their problems. The author clearly demonstrates the crisis implications to small businesses by using personal research and real-life examples in addition to a big bibliography from renowned academics. The book contains useful and practical information for small business owners, entrepreneurs from all industries, business students, academics and strategists, and business coaches and can be used as a road map during turbulent periods for small business in all industries.

The text covers the topic from different approaches, giving a bird's-eye view of contemporary trends and new approaches. Several concepts like risk management, blue ocean strategy, and turnaround management are discussed, in order to create a crystal clear understanding of why there is no such thing as dead end for small businesses—even under the worst possible situations—and how businesses can achieve sustainable development and grow.

This book was inspired by the significant problems that small and medium enterprises faced during the last huge global financial crisis.

Keywords

small business; crisis; blue ocean strategy; risk management; strategy; company culture; entrepreneur; management; financing; sustainable development

Contents

Preface

The main reason why I decided to write this book was because while I was living in Greece during the big financial years, I was in top managerial and C-suite positions in several SMEs (small-to-medium enterprise). This fact per se was enough to help me understand what I was studying during my MBA years, which was that SMEs are very important for every society, especially during turbulent times. Their survival under such difficult circumstances was the cornerstone upon which the survival of the Greek middle class, thus society as a whole, was based.

Another thing that I understood was that SMEs carry many pathogens, which when things are not going well can be huge impediments toward their sustainable development. As I was working in the banking sector for many years, I was addicted in seeing things from the banking perspective, which is the lender's one. My voluntary retirement from the last bank I was working for and my employment in several SMEs in many different industries like automotive, apparel and fashion, software, start-ups etc., made me see things from a different perspective from that of the SMEs. This was a life changer for me as it made me understand so many things, especially during the last big financial crisis that devastated Greece. This is when I started to understand better the way SMEs were trying to deal with their liquidity problems, the same ones that they are facing during normal periods and which during turbulent times become huge and difficult to deal with, as banks decrease or even stop their financing toward them.

I believe in the power of small business, and I really feel that their spirit is the entrepreneurial one.

I really hope that my experience combined with knowledge and my literature research will be a valuable guide for all enterprises, SMEs or not, in order to help them avoid certain pitfalls or potential others and guide their business toward their sustainable development. I also believe that this book will be a valuable guide in the hands of academics and business students as it contains, in a concise way, knowledge and experience on many topics that can give them a thorough picture of how SMEs can survive in their struggle during turbulent periods like the last global financial crisis.

Finally, I wanted to add that one of the more important parts of the book is the subchapter which deals with company culture. I wanted, from the beginning, to pass the message that all companies need to focus more on their human resources. Especially during difficult times, people are the ones who will be willing to lift the heavy weight of the company's successful operation. In order to do that they just need to be respected, to work in a mentally healthy environment, and to be educated on everything that has to do with their professional and personal evolvement. If they are treated well and are allowed to work in a great environment that offers them respect and safety, if they will feel part of the team and that their opinion is valued, if they feel that their ideas can be heard and that they can express them, they will be able to deliver even better and the results will be exquisite.

My humble advice to all small business owners is, treat your employees well and create an amazing company culture to which everybody will want to participate. In that way, everybody will want to work with you and the ones that already do will offer you so much more via their performance. If you acquire such mentality, your company's sustainable development, even during crisis periods, will be very close. So, let people be the epicenter of your business.

Acknowledgments

I was able to conclude this book only with the help of God and my family's love, tolerance, and understanding, so I want to thank them from the bottom of my heart.

I also want to thank the BEP team who helped me, trusted me, and gave me the opportunity to make it happen.

SECTION I

Introduction to the Small Business Concept

What is small business? Small businesses and their societal impact/small business corporate social responsibility. Small business and environmental concerns as part of their corporate social responsibility.

CHAPTER 1

Small Business: Touching Base

We all are familiar with what we call small business. It can be found everywhere as it is the pillar upon which all societies are based. According to the European Union (EU) recommendation 2003/361, the main factors that characterize a business as small and medium enterprise (SME) are the staff headcount and either the turnover or balance sheet total (ec. europa.eu, n.d., cited in Karaoulanis 2017).

1.1   What Is Small Business?

So, let's see how we can categorize a small business. The medium-sized businesses have staff <250, turnover ≤€50 m, balance sheet total ≤€43 m; small size businesses have staff <50, turnover ≤€10 m, balance sheet total ≤€10 m; micro-businesses have staff <10, turnover ≤€2 m, balance sheet total ≤€2 m (ec.europa.eu, n.d., cited in Karaoulanis 2017). Table 1.1 lists the ways that we use in order to categorize SMEs.

Table 1.1. SME characteristics

Type of Business	Staff	Turnover	Balance Sheet
Medium	<250	≤€50 m	≤€43 m
Small	<50	≤€10 m	≤€10 m
Micro	<10	≤€2 m	≤€2 m

Source: ec.europa.eu, n.d., cited in Karaoulanis (2017).

SMEs rely heavily on state support to not only operate but also try to develop and sustain their development, even during turbulent times (Romanescu 2016). For example, in the majority of countries in the EU, both the economic development and the rise of their markets are mainly supported by the application of laws and institutions implemented by the government of each country and by programs that support SMEs as their main goal (Romanescu 2016).

This is very important as it is indicative of how states perceive the important role of SMEs to society as a whole. It is also crucial here to underline that one of the biggest financing sources of SMEs is from the banking sector. Here, the state comes to play a very important role. Through specific "small business-centric" laws the state acts as the go-between and tries to establish the right operation of this transaction between the banking sector and SMEs.

1.2   The Importance of Small Businesses and Their Societal Impact

But why are SMEs so important to society? Why is their role so important? The numbers are indicative of the magnitude of their presence on a global level. The World Bank (n.d.) indicates that SMEs are the cornerstone of economies on a global scale, especially in developing countries. In emerging economies, the formal SMEs' contribution in total employment is up to 60 percent and up to 40 percent in national income (GDP),[1] while if informal SMEs are going to be included, these numbers will be raised significantly (The World Bank n.d.). It is impressive to notice here that in the next 15 years, 600 million new jobs will be needed to be created in order to absorb the continuous growth of the world's workforce. Mainly in Asia and in sub-Saharan Africa, and in emerging markets SMEs will be responsible for the creation of four out of five new positions (The World Bank n.d.).

According to the Office of the United States Trade Representative (n.d.), SMEs are the backbone of both the American and the European economies. In the United States, there are 30 million SMEs that provide two thirds of net new private sector jobs in recent decades. Of them, almost 300,000 SMEs export in foreign markets (Office of the United States Trade Representative n.d.). From these numbers, we can understand how important the role of SMEs is in the biggest economy of the world, the United States one.

---

[1]GDP: Gross Domestic Product: Is the broadest quantitative measure of a nation's total economic activity as it represents the monetary value that all the goods that are produced in a country's territory have during a specific period of time, usually annually (investinganswers.com n.d.).

Other factors that are indicative of the importance of SMEs on economic level are that they contribute to the establishment and growth of private property, they take part in both development and implementation innovations, and they participate in exports, something which is a very important factor of economic growth and which in a way can be seen as an investment attraction (Romanescu 2016).

In general, small businesses are considered to be an important paragon that affects growth and development of any economy as they play a key role in employment creation and in innovation, not to mention that their entire economic and social presence are widely recognized (Storey 1994, cited in Tse and Soufani 2003).

One can easily understand from the above that SMEs' sustainable development is crucial for the whole world. As the Organization for Economic Co-operation and Development (OECD) (2004, cited in Aksoy 2017) indicates, SMEs play a crucial role in the economies around the globe due to their huge number and the significant part of the workforce that is involved with them.

Romanescu (2016) stresses that SMEs are very important for the countries for several reasons: because they boost competition; they present the agility to help them respond to the rapidly changing demand due to globalization; they help citizens toward their self-realization, as they consist the majority of business; they provide the majority of the employment, especially during crisis years, something which is representative of their huge positive social impact, especially during such difficult periods when societies need, literally, every help they can get.

The importance of SMEs on a global level is unquestionable. Their presence has vast impact in generating the circumstances that are able to impact almost every level of the social and economic life of each country. In simple words, without small business the whole global economy will collapse and the social web as we know it will be devastated!

Another important parameter that needs to be taken into consideration is also the local character of the small business. Such character is a crucial paragon in terms of employees' organizational commitment. Under this prism SMEs that are locally owned were found to have the highest such commitment (Halbesleben and Tolbert 2014). Halbesleben and Tolbert (2014) also underline that small businesses, and especially the locally owned ones, are organized in a way that they have as part of their goals to promote and sustain the so-called social capital development that is formed as a combination of trust, communication, and concern about others' well-being within interpersonal relationships, which in our case spring from the closer bond that can be found in local societies. This strong social character of local SMEs is extremely important and plays a vital role in the local societies.

Local communities are based heavily on the advancement and growth of SMEs, especially in decentralized areas where SMEs are the only kind of companies that exist. No matter whether SMEs are locally owned or not, their importance to local societies is huge. They act like a barometer. Anything that will have a negative impact to them will be followed by an even larger negative impact to their local society as a whole.

Karaoulanis (2016) did a case study on the ethical consequences in the decision-making process that might take place in small business in Greece during the years of the last financial crisis. The company that was examined was an SME that operated in the textile industry in Greece and which due to the turbulence of the last financial crisis that heavily struck Greece had to take a major decision, which was to move its operations to a neighboring country which was more favorable for SMEs, commercial and tax laws. The company in question was based in a small town populated with about 60,000 people. The ethical dilemma that the owners had to answer was going to have a vast impact in the local society, not only due to the fact that the majority of the company's employees were living in the local society but also because a variety of other small businesses were also operating in collaboration (suppliers, contractors etc.) with the SME in question. Inevitably they were going to lose their grip in the local market—something which eventually would lead them to bankruptcy (Karaoulanis 2016). The above-mentioned phenomenon was not the only one in Greece during this period of time. In fact a huge number of companies still are into this process of relocating to neighboring countries, even as we speak, about ten years after the outbreak of the economic crisis.

The bond between SMEs and local societies is extremely important and has a vast impact in people's well-being and societal balance. This is why the role of SMEs under such circumstances is huge, and the ethical dilemmas that SMEs' owners sometimes need to confront are huge as well.

So, as SMEs have a very strong connection with the local societies and their mutual existence is based upon this factor, they need to increase their corporate social responsibility (CSR) in order to meet the local societies' needs and to cultivate the notion that they are there not only to increase their revenue but also to help and to grow together, hand in hand with the local societies. They need to make these very local societies to understand that SMEs are a vital part of them and that their mutual existence is bonded in a powerful and bidirectional way.

Another very important paragon that is a determinant of the level of SMEs contribution to the society is that they create the conditions needed in order to help toward the formation of the middle class, something which is the cornerstone of the stability on a societal level (Romanescu 2016). Romanescu (2016) also adds that SMEs have the ability to boost competition, something which has huge importance in the economic growth of societies. The increased competition on a local level can result in lower prices for the consumers, and more companies to compete with each other, something which will increase the number of job opportunities that will be filled by the locals as well in a big majority.

CSR is a concept that is often heard in the business scenery of all countries and industries. CSR is considered to be the moral, ethical, and philanthropic responsibilities that organizations have in addition to their core responsibility, which is to earn a fair return on investment to their shareholders while they are obliged to comply with law and regulations posed by the government or the international law (Campopiano, De Massis, and Cassia 2012). In this way of thinking, organizations need to approach their responsibilities in a broader way in order to include not only their shareholders but also their employees, suppliers, customers, the local community, the local and national governments, and other groups of special interest (Campopiano, De Massis, and Cassia 2012).

According to Murillo and Lozano (2006, cited in Campopiano, De Massis, and Cassia 2012), SMEs have specific characteristics that play an important role in terms of their commitment and engagement toward their CSR. Such characteristics present a heterogeneous spectrum of sizes, which starts from the so-called micro-SMEs and continues to the medium and large ones (Campopiano, De Massis, and Cassia 2012). SMEs also have a strong bond between the environment and the communities in which they operate (Murillo and Lozano 2006, cited in Campopiano, De Massis, and Cassia 2012), while entrepreneurs-owners pay a lot of attention to the interpersonal relationships (Murillo and Lozano 2006, cited in Campopiano, De Massis, and Cassia 2012).

In addition, another important distinct characteristic which makes special the way SMEs approach their CSR is that entrepreneurs-owners are usually sensitive to all the activities that have an important impact to their stakeholders with whom they are in a direct connection, like employees, customers, and suppliers in a way that they lead their small business to implement a responsible behavior toward that direction, as they perceive such behavior as a way of good management approach (Fassin, 2008, cited in Campopiano, De Massis, and Cassia 2012).

But is CSR something that can be found in SMEs or is it something that has to do only with large corporations? Corporate Social Responsibility (CSR) is a term that we hear mainly when large firms are involved. According to Berk (2017), for many SMEs, such term is something that is not very well accepted or even not well enough understood. This is why the term seems to be unattractive for many SMEs, even when they are actually engaging in such activities (Giovanna and Lucio 2012; Jenkins 2006; Lee and Pang 2012, cited in Berk 2017).

The different ways in which small and large businesses comprehend and approach the CSR made scholars to coin a new term which applies specifically to small business and is the "small business social responsibility" (SBSR) (Lepoutre and Heene 2006; Spence 2015, cited in Berk 2017). According to Soundararajan et al. (2016, cited in Berk 2017), the new term is defined as the activities that small companies are engaged in and which are result in creating a positive change in the society.

Although small companies are engaged in CSR activities, it is not easy to gather information about them when we deal with large companies which publish reports and in general make easier for the interested parties to be able to find such information publicly and especially online (Fassin 2008; Wickert et al. 2016, cited in Berk 2017).

Berk's (2017) research on 2,653 small businesses in the USA concluded that small businesses have a high level of participation in CSR activities, while parameters like SMEs, leadership, and employees are playing a vital role in SMEs' CSR activities/engagement.

In addition to the above-mentioned indications regarding the CSR of small business, Lepoutre and Heene (2006) state that small businesses in general will face more barriers than large ones while trying to exercise their actions toward CSR. Such barriers will be faced with regard to the companies' external stakeholders or the natural environment (Lepoutre and Heene 2006). This might be one of the main reasons why CSR is not so often encountered in small businesses as in larger ones.

Since small businesses might face such barriers, a very important step that needs to be taken toward the overcoming of such obstacles is the actions adapted by the small business owners-managers (Lepoutre and Heene 2006). This is why, SME owners need to become more effective in their actions toward their company's SBSR activities, for example, by seeking partnerships in the market where their companies are operating, in the government, in the very society which they want to help, or in the entire supply chain, toward the common goal of alleviating societal problems (Lepourte and Heene 2006). Via such initiatives and partnerships they will be able to develop the needed capabilities in order to overcome the barriers that might prevent them from implementing the SBSR actions which the society in which they operate needs (Lepourte and Heene 2006).

Another important role that SMEs play in the society is their environmental impact. Although several studies showed that formal managerial tools, such as environmental reporting or ISO 14001, are not the most suitable ones for utilization among SMEs (Graafland and Smid 2016), SME managers' awareness of such tools (Johnson 2013 cited in Graafland and Smid 2016) and awareness raising programs for SMEs are possibly the best ways that can be used in order to help SMEs adopt more environmental management tools (Bradford and Fraser 2008 cited in Graafland and Smid 2016).

According to Roy and Therin (2008, cited in Graafland and Smid 2016), there are two main kinds of organizations that can help SMEs the most toward that direction: the industrial organizations and the trade ones. As such organizations are better informed about the environmental circumstances by their members, they can help SMEs by transmitting to them the information needed in order to help them adapt the environmental tools they need toward their positive environmental impact (Roy and Therin 2008 cited in Graafland and Smid 2016).

SMEs are usually kept back from their environmental targets due to their "natural" constraints which are unanimous to their very existence, such as lack of time, lack of finances and lack of knowledge in the specific area (Roy and Therin 2008 cited in Graafland and Smid 2016). With the help of the above-mentioned two kinds of organizations, SMEs will be able to develop their environment-oriented managerial tools, in other words, they could be able to overcome their embedded "natural" deficiencies and reach their goal in terms of their environmental impact to the society in which they operate (Roy and Therin 2008 cited in Graanfland and Smid 2016).

Such managerial tools are mainly informal, while they can become more formal when the SMEs in question will be on tracks. In that way such tools can help SMEs even more in terms of achieving an even better environmental impact (Roy and Therin 2008 cited in Graanfland and Smid 2016).

In terms of SMEs' environmental considerations, Menguc et al. (2009, cited in Arend 2014) argued that the SMEs' entrepreneurial orientation (EO) and CSR and/or their "going green" approach are interrelated, something which in plain words means that SMEs can become more "green" in order to be able to have a stronger presence in terms of implementing their CSR in a profitable way, especially without formalization and in a way that will be beneficial for both the society and their shareholders.

Stoian and Gilman (2017) argue that by aligning SMEs' CSR activities with a company's competitive strategic approach, growth not only can be achieved but also can be enhanced. Stoian and Gilman (2017) also in their survey between 211 U.K.-based SMEs found that CSR activities that are focused on the society are paragons that increase the company's growth and that CSR which is mainly focused on the company's personnel are extremely important in helping the SMEs in question to avoid possible decline in sales, mainly in companies that are focused in a differentiation approach or in a quality-focused strategic one.

On the contrary, Stoian and Gilman (2017) stress that when CSR is focused on environmental issues, it is not beneficial for the SME in terms of helping it increase its growth, while when CSR activities are more focused on human rights-related issues they can even slow growth, especially when the small company in question is adopting or trying to adopt a differentiation or a quality-focused strategy (Stoian and Gilman 2017). Of course, small businesses need to understand that even if there might be several negative outcomes in the short run, their environmental and even their human rights approach will be beneficial in the long run, as it will be able to establish a very strong brand name for them as the customer will realize that they really care and that they have a sensitive face.

We can see from what Stoian and Gilman (2017) and Graanfland and Smid (2016) stress that the role of CSR with an environmental focus can be quite a controversial topic, something which can be found in literature worldwide. The paragon that makes the difference and can make the environmental approach of the specific CSR activities of SMEs to positively contribute to the company's growth in combination with the increase of the company's impact on a societal level is the impact due to the "collaboration" between SMEs and industrial and trade organizations as Roy and Therin (2008, cited in Graaflnad and Smid 2016) argued.

As small businesses are a crucial paragon in terms of everybody's prosperity on a global level, their survival, especially during crisis years, is of the outmost importance. The adaptation of CSR and their environment-focused operations, although for some, might feel like they will have a negative impact in their profits in the short run, but in the long run will help them not only to survive but also to have a positive impact to the society as a whole, something which will enhance their brand name and will retain their customers. Toward that direction small businesses need to take the right actions which always will spring from their owners' approach toward such parameters. Especially when small businesses are locally based, their impact to the local societies is vast and this is why their survival and their decisions in general will affect not only them, but their local surroundings as well. This is another extremely important paragon that needs to be taken into consideration by the SMEs' owners as well.

Author's Notes

In this chapter, we presented a general view about SMEs: what they are, how they can be categorized, and what impact they have on societies worldwide.

The main points that we need to be focused on are the following:
- The small business classification into categories.
- The societal impact of SMEs on both local and global levels.

In terms of the societal impact of SMEs, the main points that we need to focus on are the following:

- They are the cornerstone of all economies.
- They have a wide local character, which drives employees' commitment.
- They create the conditions needed toward the formation of the middle class, something which provides stability to the society as a whole.
- They have a vast societal impact via their CSR actions.
- They have important environmental impact.

Another very interesting point that is good to be discussed is the SMEs' owners' attitude via several perspectives, like strategy, company culture, societal implications, etc.

Suggested Questions:
1. What are the main characteristics of small businesses? How can they be categorized and in what way?
2. Why is small business' societal impact a very important paragon? What are their main contributions to society as a whole?
3. What is and should be the small business owners' attitude toward important business parameters like strategy, company culture, and social implications?

4. Do you believe that SMEs' environmental focus can be a positive or a negative paragon in terms of affecting the company's growth? What are your thoughts, especially nowadays when humanity is facing major environmental problems?

This first section is very important as it helps students' engagement with the books' topic. By understanding what SMEs are and how they impact society, they will be able to understand what they see around them on a daily basis, that is, entrepreneurs trying to establish their local small business in their very neighborhood. That will make them curious and hopefully they will begin to see things around them from a different perspective. They will also be able to understand the contents of the rest of the book and why SME survival during crisis years is so important, not only for them but for the whole society as well.

CHAPTER 2

A Depiction of Small Business from an Entrepreneurial Approach

Small business' entrepreneurial orientation (innovativeness, proactiveness, and risk-taking mentality). Owners' mind-set/entrepreneurial characteristics. The three pillars of entrepreneurship. Market orientation. Small business' strategic management.

2.1 Small Business and Entrepreneurial Orientation

In a constantly and rapidly changing world, small business and entrepreneurial orientations (SMEs) need to be on their toes to sustain and develop. As discussed in Chapter 1, the survival of SMEs is of utmost importance for the society as a whole.

One of the most important parameters to be considered is the environment in which SMEs need to operate today—a global business environment characterized by the shortening of both product and business model life cycles and which makes future profit from today's operations to be uncertain, which inevitably results in business constantly seeking for new opportunities (Hamel 2000, cited in Wiklund et al. 2005). This is why SMEs need to reconsider whether they need to adapt an EO or not. To endure the fierce competition and the rapidly changing environment, SMEs need to adapt an EO (Aloulou and Fayolle 2005). Innovativeness, reactiveness, and risk-taking are three main attributes that comprise the EO mentality (Aloulou and Fayolle 2005).

But what is EO? According to Lumpkin and Dess (1996, cited in Wiklund et al. 2005), EO mainly refers to a firm's strategic orientation by underlying specific aspects of entrepreneurial behavior such as decision-making styles, methods used, and practices followed. In other words, it mainly refers to how a firm operates, rather than what it does.

For SMEs it is crucial to adapt an EO mentality, because in that way they will achieve better results via a new approach in terms of their operations, an approach which seems to be quite dynamic and resourceful. The combination of reactiveness, innovation, and risk-taking is indicative of how EO operates in any global environment (Figure 2.1). These very characteristics are the ones that will make the difference when the situations are difficult to deal with and will decide the SME's future in the short and the long run.

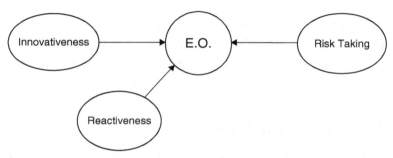

Figure 2.1 The three main attributes that comprise the EO mentality
Source: Aloulou and Fayolle (2005).

SMEs nowadays are deemed to operate in a globalized environment. In addition, the Internet has shaped a completely different global market in which customers have access to multiple markets and an incredible amount of information in seconds. This information asymmetry between small business and their customers has dramatically been reversed the last years. The result of this globalization and this change in customers' "power" is that SMEs need to compete with each other in a race that is hard to win, as the competition is fierce, while they have to deal with more "educated" customers with increased awareness in terms of the offered products.

Kraus et al. (2012) agree that due to globalization, SMEs are facing fierce competition worldwide. In addition the change in how customers think, react, decide, and eventually buy makes apparent that SMEs are facing increasing difficulty in maintaining and improving their business results in time, unless they can find a solution in terms of how to handle the abovementioned pressures (Kraus et al. 2012).

The Internet changed the global buying landscape dramatically in the last years and accordingly, customers' behavior. In just a few minutes customers can check the same product and its price from all over the world. Although amazing, it has changed the equilibrium between the seller and the customer. Customers have huge info power in their hands, this being the case only since the last 10–20 years on a global scale. This fact per se, as Kraus et al. (2012) underlined in the previous paragraph, is something that SMEs should not take lightly.

An entrepreneurial mind-set can be used by SMEs as a yardstick to survival by the recognition of both the threats and the opportunities of their surrounding environment (Krueger 2000, cited in Kraus et al. 2012), especially during crisis years when the competition is even greater and the markets seem saturated.

The entrepreneurial mind-set is a powerful weapon in the hands of SMEs' owners. But as Shiraishi and Barbosa (2015) indicate, this very mind-set, in terms of how to be used in the form of ideas which will be translated into strategies, is one of the biggest challenges SME owners face.

The ability of SME owners to materialize their ideas into strategy within a formal organizational structure is not something easy and very often important knowledge about business strategy remains in the owner's mind without being disseminated in any way to SME stakeholders, partners, employees, friends, or even family members (Shiraishi and Barbosa 2015). This phenomenon is fatal in terms of hindering the chances of business growth, business model replication, not to mention the successful succession in family business, something which is very common as regards SMEs (Shiraishi and Barbosa 2015).

Although SME owners need to develop an entrepreneurial mind-set, such procedure is not easy and entails situations by which the whole concept makes the mind-set's implementation and usage something that on the bottom line do not help business at all. A big portion of how this mentality can be implemented is in the hands of SME owners who need to embrace it in order to be able to implement it on a company level and in the right way.

The next important problem that occurs when dealing with SMEs is that their owners often don't have the mind-set needed to adopt to one of the most important paragons that affect strategy—their surrounding environment (Shiraishi and Barbosa 2015). Without such ability it is inevitable to not implement not only the right strategy but also to plan the right organizational structure in order to help them manage the company in a more easy, structured, and efficient way (Shiraishi and Barbosa 2015). As a result, performance could be lower than expected, not to mention that many times such attitudes might create a generation gap between SME owners and their offspring, as the majority of SMEs are family owned. In that case, when they come to management, the owners' children tend to accuse their parents that they were narrow-minded and that they created a situation under which it is very difficult for them to handle the whole organization (Shiraishi and Barbosa 2015). This is something that will create operational and morality problems to the new SME owners and will jeopardize the whole company's growth in the long run.

Also SME owners although sometimes are very experienced entrepreneurs and have an in-depth knowledge of the market, they find it quite difficult to transform this knowledge and experience into strategy formulation in a way that their company will be benefited in both the short and the long run (Shiraishi and Barbosa 2015). As this is a crucial point for the whole business operation, especially when things are difficult and there is no space for wrong movements in terms of strategy implementation, a solution needs to be given. Shiraishi and Barbosa (2015) propose a five-step procedure that needs to be used in order to bridge that gap and bring the right equilibrium in small business by enhancing the SME owners' capabilities to produce the right ideas and reincarnate them into strategy. Shiraishi and Barbosa (2015) describe the five steps as follows:

- Identify all the macro environments and the specific competitive context in which the company had exposure till now.
- Via the use of in-depth interviews we need to identify all the important milestones in the SME owner's life.
- In order to understand the owner's motives, we need to reconstruct both the life of the owner and her business time frame by emphasizing key events, environmental and personal changes, specific

strategic actions, and their negative and positive consequences. Under this prism, we need to create a time frame which will include the whole concept of the abovementioned milestones of both the company and the owner.

- A second round of in-depth interviews is needed to validate the given time frame and to evoke the strategic decisions made at each key moment of her personal and professional life.

- It is important that during revisiting the abovementioned key moments of both the business and the owner, we need to explore where and when there is convergence and/or divergence between the decisions and the choices made, both in the personal and in the professional level.

According to Blackburn, Hart, and Wainwright (2013), the size and the age of the company are the most dominant factors in terms of performance to such degree that they need to be considered as more important factors than the entrepreneurial characteristics[1] of the SME's owner, **as we can see them depicted in** figure 2.2.

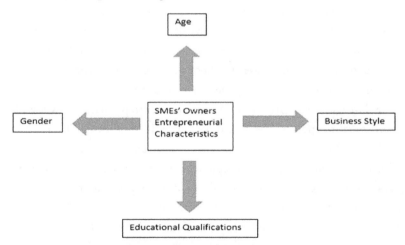

Figure 2.2 SME owners' entrepreneurial characteristics

Source: Blackburn, Hart, and Wainwright (2013)

---

[1]Owners' entrepreneurial characteristics: They are, the age of the owners/managers, the gender composition of the owners, the educational qualifications of the business owners, and the owners' business style (Blackburn, Hart and Wainwright 2013).

As Stevenson and Gumpert (1991, cited in Thurik and Wennekers 2004) stress, entrepreneurship is a way of behaving, which concentrates mainly on opportunities rather than on resources, as we can encounter such behavior trends in both small and large businesses and elsewhere.

The entrepreneurial mind-set is an important factor for all companies. Entrepreneurs need to be open-minded and discover opportunities where others can only find problems. This mind-set is the one that SME owners need to have in order to be able to break through, especially during difficult periods of time, like during recession years, or when markets are saturated. This kind of mentality will be the one that will implement the blue ocean strategy and will help the company to survive by inventing new market spaces, as will be seen in Chapter 5.

In parallel, Wennekers and Thurik (1999, cited in Thurik and Wennekers 2004) underline that the entrepreneurial role in economic development is paramount mainly via the innovation it introduces (Schumpeterian entrepreneurship).[2] Under this prism, SMEs can be run not only by the use of this kind of entrepreneurial activities, but also by people who simply run and own a small business for living (Thurik and Wennekers 2004). This group of people which consists of shopkeepers, franchisees, and ones in several other professional occupations belongs to what Kirchhoff (1994, cited in Thurik and Wennekers 2004) coined as the "economic core." They are the heart of the society, the heart of the neighborhood. They are a vivid part of each society's middle class and this is why they are so important.

Sahut and Peris-Ortiz (2014) stress that entrepreneurship is mainly based on three pillars. The first one (North 1990; Scott 2007, cited in Sahut and Peris-Ortiz 2014) is the law involved and the rules of the game, which means the rules that entrepreneurs follow inside the specific market's constrains of a market. This factor is extremely important and can be the decisive paragon for entrepreneurs in general and SME owners specifically when they will be in a position to consider, that is, in which country they want to operate their business (see Chapter 1).

---

[2]In 1934 Schumpeter introduced a theory according to which entrepreneurs as individuals have, among other things, to produce new combinations of resources. They also have the eye to identify and implement new opportunities that arise in the economy. This is why their role in economic growth is paramount (Ferreira et al. 2017).

The second pillar is about the values and the rules that spring from such values as social, organizational, individual, and customs (Bruton et al. 2010; March and Olsen 1989; Scott 2007, cited in Sahut and Peris-Ortiz 2014).

Finally, the third pillar refers to deeper beliefs and values which influence the entrepreneur without them being aware of such influence anyway (Bandura 1986; Bruton et al. 2010; Carroll 1964; Scott 2007, cited in Sahut and Peris-Ortiz 2014).

These three pillars are extremely important and need to be taken under much consideration from any businesses that want to sustain in both the short and the long run. Small businesses which are guided by owners who have the right skill set and the right entrepreneurial mind-set need to be focused in such direction. Taking any of these pillars lightly can be fatal for small business.

Although entrepreneurship and small business have many things in common, there are several things that create a differentiation between the two concepts.

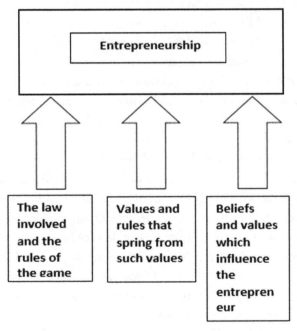

Figure 2.3 The three pillars of entrepreneurship (Sahut and Peris-Ortiz 2014)

According to Carland et al. (1984), one of the most important of these differentiation factors is that although entrepreneurial ventures can start as a small business, they continue to grow over time. Of course small businesses can grow over time as well, but many of them continue to be small with the passage of time (Carland et al. 1984).

Growth is crucial for small business, especially during turbulent times when the majority of businesses, regardless of their size, tend to shrink; so small businesses need to adapt an entrepreneurial mentality, which mainly should spring from their owners' mentality. Besides innovativeness, SMEs owners' mentality is a very important paragon that can help small business in multiple ways.

Carland et al. (1984) try to underline that not all new ventures are entrepreneurial in nature and that the critical factor that distinguishes entrepreneurs from managers who are not into real entrepreneurial mentality is innovation. Innovation is a factor that affects small business extremely heavily as will be seen in the following chapters. The innovative mind-set is also a very important part of the blue ocean strategy that we will examine in Chapter 5 and is a factor that can drastically help entrepreneurs, and especially SME owners, to move away from dangerous situations and to overcome difficult ones. This is true especially during crisis years, as it can help businesses materialize their competitive advantage and compete in a victorious way with their opponents toward survival.

As small businesses have specific characteristics that differentiate them from entrepreneurship as a whole, the same holds for entrepreneurs and small business owners.

After analyzing a sample of 194 business owners in the hospitality industry, Wagener, Gorgievski, and Rijsdijk (2010) concluded that there are several characteristics that discriminate small business owners from entrepreneurs. The authors underlined that entrepreneurs possessed higher levels of some characteristics like tolerance in terms of ambiguity, independence, non-risk aversion attitude, innovativeness, and leadership, while they possessed equal levels of market awareness/orientation and self-efficacy. This example from the hospitality industry is a very prominent one in terms of creating two ways in approaching things between entrepreneurs and small business owners—one that unifies their attitudes and characteristics and another which separates them.

Wennekers and Thurik (1999, cited in Thurik and Wennekers 2004) argue that small businesses are the backbone of society as they contribute to employment and social and political stability. In a way, we witnessed a shift for small businesses from a social good that needed to be maintained at any cost to small businesses as a way of exercising entrepreneurship, which is considered as a vital determinant of economic growth (Audretsch and Thurik 2000; Audretsch et al. 2001, 2002b; Carree and Thurik 1999; Carree et al. 2002, cited in Thurik and Wennekers 2004).

This occurs as small businesses tend to remain small as time goes by. This is not something negative but it is a choice that needs to be made by entrepreneurs, or do we need to say by small business owners? Although there is a blurred thin line between the two notions, it is crucial to underline here that the mentality of an entrepreneur who starts as a small business owner but has in mind to expand and grow, and a small business owner who starts as a small business owner and remains that way forever, is completely different.

We can conclude that although SMEs have some differences in terms of operations and mentality from large business and entrepreneurship as a whole, they can be perceived as an integral part of entrepreneurship. As such, they need to have embedded the so-called entrepreneurial spirit. In fact, such spirit needs to be the cornerstone and the yardstick toward development. As some SMEs suffer from the lack of such spirit, this fact is naturally then depicted in the way their owners approach things, not to mention that it is also depicted in their results and development throughout time.

In the contemporary global market, small businesses also need to consider factors such as risk. Although one of their main characteristics is that they are risk averse, they need to have in mind how to face risk and to manipulate it in a way that it can be beneficial or at least will not damage them in the short and in the long run as well.

A very characteristic example of how SMEs perceive their relationship with risk can be vividly depicted in Karaoulanis's (2017) research, which was conducted in numerous Greek SMEs in order to examine their risk management mechanisms and the impediments that they were facing due to the lack of financing and the capital controls that were imposed by the Greek government. The results of this qualitative research indicated that small business owners don't use sophisticated risk management mechanisms, while some don't use such mechanisms at all. This is indicative of the abovementioned situation as the lack of risk management mechanisms and can be considered as the result of the lack of the entrepreneurial spirit of SME owners. So, we can understand how SMEs facing risk is something which characterizes them and in many ways differentiates them from the entrepreneurial mind-set which can be found in bigger businesses.

Another paragon which is quite important in SMEs' entrepreneurial way of operating is the leadership style that small business owners exercise. It is a paragon that can be crucial in terms of how SMEs operate and especially in terms of how SMEs can blend their small business mentality with the entrepreneurial one. Domingo Ribeiro Soriano and José Manuel Comeche Martínez (2007) conducted a study which was focused in establishing results toward discovering the influence of specific variables involved in specific leadership styles. The study indicated that such variables are the basis of the implementation and maintenance of an entrepreneurial spirit inside the very SMEs' culture on a work team level, throughout the SME.

The abovementioned research which was based on personal interviews and a LISREL 8 analysis[3] pinpointed that the leadership style is a factor of huge importance as, when it was based on relationships, it had more than double influence power than a participating leadership (Soriano and Martínez 2007).

A task-oriented leadership style found that it was reducing the chances of transmitting the entrepreneurial spirit to the working team, thus was not able to create a so-called collective entrepreneurial spirit, something which is a very important factor in terms of helping the SME in question to develop leadership in the long run (Soriano and Martínez 2007).

The connection between EO and SMEs' performance has been investigated extensively to date, as it is very important to understand that if SMEs will be able to exercise an EO, they will be benefited in multiple

---

[3]LISREL analysis: LISREL is an acronym (Linear Structural Relations). It refers either to structural equation modeling or to Joreskog and Sorbom's statistical computer software program which can be used to test such models (Joreskog and Sorbom 1996a; Joreskog, Sorbom, du Toit, and du Toi 2000, cited in Anagnostopoulos, n.d.).

ways and they will be able to increase their performance toward growth. In their research regarding the possible connection between EO and SME performance, Wiklund et al. (2005) concluded that EO positively influences SME performance, although such performance is always influenced by other paragons too, like access to financial capital, the environmental influence, etc. What is important here though is that SME owners who can adapt the so-called entrepreneurial orientation can assist their companies' operations in a more efficient way, not to mention that they will be able to respond to any challenges that will appear in a more successful way.

2.2   Factors Affecting the Small Business' Performance

To understand on a deeper level how SMEs operate, it is imperative first to understand which paragons are involved in business generally and accordingly in SMEs too in terms of affecting positively their overall performance. Peter Drucker once said, "Culture eats strategy for breakfast" and this is a huge truth. Organizational culture is an extremely important paragon involved in business. It is not involved only in large companies; it is equally involved and is of utmost importance in small businesses as well (Baker and Sinkula 2009). This is why SMEs need to be able to adopt the right culture and use it as a powerful weapon that will boost productivity and give them a huge competitive advantage.

Aside from the organizational culture, another very important factor which is involved in the small business' success, besides the EO in previous paragraphs, is Market Orientation[4] (MO; Baker and Sinkula 2009).

Baker and Sinkula (2009) underline that MO and EO are two extremely important parameters that are involved in SMEs' profitability. In fact, a very important point of correlation between them is that both approaches prioritize learning about customers and markets (Baker and Sinkula 2009).

---

[4]Market Orientation (MO): Refers to the extent to which companies value that much of their customer's needs and wants as one of their primary organizing principles giving them a leading role (Jawoski and Kohli 1993, cited in Baker and Sinkula 2009).

Wiklund and Shepherd (2003) approached the whole concept in the same direction. Their 2015 research findings pinpoint a main paragon that is involved in a straight line with firm performance, thus increasing profitability—the use of knowledge-based resources[5]—and that EO enhances such relationship (Wiklund and Shepherd 2003).

Knowledge-based resources are crucial in business development, especially during turbulent periods of time, as they are the means that need to be used in order to help SMEs discover and exploit new opportunities. It is obvious that without EO, knowledge-based resources will be used less or even won't be used at all. This is very indicative of the correlation between entrepreneurial spirit/mentality and how SMEs need to operate.

Having their customers in the epicenter of their strategy consists of a very positive, toward-innovation approach. It is very natural to try to be innovative while seeking to reach your customer's need and wants. In contrast, being innovative helps SMEs to be competitive and even acquire a strong competitive advantage against their rivals. There are many paradigms of such approach. "Customers as innovators" is one of them, which makes customers the very persons that contribute in the company's R&D (Research and Development) via their suggestions.

This approach was very disruptive when it was implemented for the first time and still can be found in many SMEs as it makes your customers a part of the team, cultivates a bond between the company and the customers, and gives the clear message that customers are the number one priority of the company in terms of the offered products. Such examples are the "build-it-yourself" products like kitchens, personal computers, etc.

According to Baker and Sinkula (2009), another important factor which is the result of strong MO in correlation with strong EO is the increase in profit margins for the SMEs in question. Such increase involves the combination of target market selection, product development and innovation, implementing the right pricing strategy, using the more effective distribution channels, the targeted promotion of the SMEs' products.

---

[5]Knowledge-Based Resources: They are resources applicable in discovering and exploiting entrepreneurial opportunities (Wiklund and Shepherd 2003).

Kajalo and Lindblom (2015) argue that MO and EO are important paragons in formulating small business performance; they need to be seen only as they act on a basic level. Their involvement with the SMEs' performance is not as straightforward as it might seem to be (Kajalo and Lindblom 2015), as in order to help SMEs increase their performance and thus profitability, they need to use marketing capabilities. In other words, marketing should be a vital component which needs to be involved with MO and EO in order to increase performance and thus profitability (Kajalo and Lindblom 2015).

The importance of MO is huge for SMEs as it helps them to establish their brand name, something which will help them also to create an authority around their name and their products. This fact per se will attract new customers and will retain the existing ones. MO will also help them promote their products or services in their targeted audience. This is extremely important as well especially nowadays, as digital marketing and social media can play a vital role in approaching customers. Targeted advertisements and remarketing are techniques that digital marketers use to help companies reach their exact targeting audience—that is, regarding its age, sex, region, etc.

Andersén et al. (2017) found that a factor of utmost importance in SMEs' performance is the correlation between EO (Entrepreneurial Orientation) and employees' well-being as a result of potential increased role ambiguity exactly due to the company's OE approach. The result was that OE and role ambiguity[6] are closely related (Andersén et al. 2017), as EO is often correlated with continuous change and renewal—characteristics that can be the root for the abovementioned role ambiguity and uncertainty (Burgeman 1985; Dess et al. 1999; Hayton 2005; Ireland et al. 1996; Lumpkin and Dess 1996; Rafferty and Griffin 2006; Wales et al. 2011, cited in Andersén et al. 2017).

Role ambiguity is a very important factor that SME owners need to consider carefully. There are several times when employees' role is not

---

[6]Role ambiguity: Role ambiguity is "a perceived lack of job related information" where with the term job related, we mean performance expectations, goals, assignments handed to the employee, authority and hierarchy, responsibilities that the employee will be assigned, etc. (Yun et al. 2007:746, cited in Andersén et al. 2017).

adequately conveyed by the managers/owners; something will usually result in decreased employee performance. Another important result might be misunderstandings between employees or between managers and employees, something that will eventually create a bad working climate that will have a negative impact on the whole company's performance.

Also, it is important for the SME owner to convey the company's mission and vision in a proper way so that everybody will be able to understand it and align his or her efforts in the same direction.

Of note is that EO tends to create a direction toward creativity and the formation of entrepreneurial capabilities among employees (Alvarez and Barney 2002, cited in Andersén et al. 2017), something which accordingly creates a loose working environment in order to make employees work under a more autonomous scheme (Hayton 2005; Lumpkin and Dess 1996, cited in Andersén et al. 2017). This can be perceived as part of the whole company culture. As company culture has a huge impact on every part of the organization, a culture which has as one of its main characteristics the OE will help employees grow toward that direction.

Although owner's–manager's characteristics and the adapted business style, as we saw in the previous paragraphs, are, among others, important paragons that are involved in the small business performance, another equally important paragon which has vast impact on small business performance is the structural conditions within which the small company operates (Blackburn, Hart, and Wainwright 2013).

What form the business might have is an important factor which can determine how the company operates. If the company is formed by only one or two persons, determining how decisions are taken, how responsibilities are contributed, and even determining the company's financial future, especially during periods of crisis, can be crucial.

2.3   Small Business and Strategy Formulation

In terms of strategy formulation, Keyvani (2011) stresses what can be considered an integral part of a three-phase strategic management[7] process,

---

[7]Strategic Management: According to Harrison 1999; McCall 1990; Porter 1980; Porter 1980, 1985; Williams 2002, cited in Keyvani 2011), strategic management is

which includes diagnosis, formulation, and implementation. Figure 2.4 depicts how a strategy can be formulated as part of the whole strategic management process.

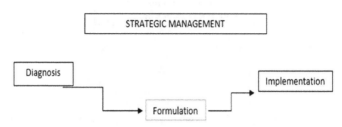

Figure 2.4 Strategy formulation as part of strategic management process (Keyvani 2011)

From the figure, one can easily understand that the whole management process moves from left to right, leading to the implementation of the strategy in question for the firm. In other words, in order for the small business company to implement the right strategy, it needs to investigate the whole situation/market and understand where it stands and in which environment it competes in order to be able to formulate its findings into a concrete strategic plan. The last step is the implementation of this plan with success.

What is strategy formulation? Keyvani (2011) underlines that strategy formulation is a very important procedure according to which companies can modify their current objectives and strategies in order to achieve the company's goals, or in other words to be able to implement a more successful strategy. We can say that strategy formulation is "responsible" for the creation of the so-called sustainable competitive advantage that the company seeks to establish in order to thrive (Keyvani 2011). Strategy formulation is the cornerstone of strategy implementation.

Verreynne and Meyer (2010) indicate that when it comes to small businesses, there are three main processes that they use in order to "make"

---

an ongoing process which has as its target to revise future oriented strategies which have been implemented by the company in order to help achieve its entrepreneurial objectives, to make the company able to consider its capabilities, its constraints, and of course the environment in which it operates as it is an important paragon as well.

strategy, the simplistic,[8] the participative,[9] and the adaptive.[10] These three approaches can be seen in Figure 2.5.

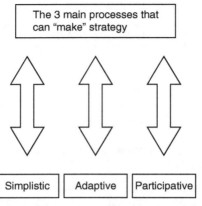

Figure 2.5 The three main processes that can "make" strategy (Verreynne and Meyer 2010)

Verreynne and Meyer (2010) continue that these approaches/processes are all related in one way or another to the small company's performance, although their importance and their impact is subject to change depending on the industry life cycle. For example, small companies that operate in mature industries are most likely to benefit from the use of the adaptive approach, while the simplistic approach is only important

[8]*Simplistic:* According to Miller (1993, cited in Verreynne and Meyer 2010), this approach focuses on factors that led the company in question to success in the past, so the repetition of these factors/actions will develop an "overwhelming preoccupation" which will be based on a single goal, specific strategic activity, department, or world view.

[9]*Participative:* Collier et al. (2004, cited in Verreynne and Meyer 2010) define the participative approach as a strategy-making approach by which both strategy and its directions on firm level are the results of the inclusion in the whole process of several points of view of internal stakeholders.

[10]*Adaptive:* Is the active engagement of external stakeholders in the decision-making process in terms of the directions and the strategies that the company adapts and adapting the strategic direction that the company will follow via the use of the market feedback (Quinn, 1980, cited in Verreynne and Meyer 2010).

in companies which operate in growth industries and only when they are used in combination with adaptive and participative strategy making approaches (Verreynne and Meyer 2010).

In conclusion, small businesses in general, and especially when they operate in turbulent environments, need to be agile enough toward solving their problems, the ones that don't leave them to grow and escape from devastation. To achieve that goal, their owners need to adapt an entrepreneurial mind-set in order to be able to implement in their companies the EO needed. Such orientation will make easier for them to follow the seven paragons described in this chapter which are responsible for the successful operation of small businesses, besides being able to implement the right strategy that the company needs in order to overcome the impediments that the crisis posed and hold it back. This is why it is so important for every small business which operates under turbulent environments in saturated markets to adapt such an EO approach.

Author's Notes

This chapter is a very important one because it gives us the opportunity not only to stress very important facts in terms of how SMEs are operating but also because it gives us the opportunity to focus on the entrepreneurial mind-set and its importance to business that SMEs are conducting, especially during financially turbulent times.

The main points on which we need to be focused on are the following:

- The SMEs' presence in global markets.
- The fierce competition that they are facing as a result of such presence and how this is a game changer.
- The SME owners' ability to materialize their ideas into strategies. Their ability to adapt an entrepreneurial mind-set.
- Small business as part of entrepreneurship as a whole.
- The paragons involved in successful operation of small businesses.
- The correlation between marketing orientation and entrepreneurial orientation and its role in SMEs' core business approach.

Suggested questions:

1. Are SMEs bound to local markets only or do they operate on a global level no matter if they want it or not? Why is this a game changer?
2. Why it is important for SME owners to adapt an entrepreneurial mind-set?
3. Which are some of the important factors that help SMEs to adapt an entrepreneurial approach and to let small business to be considered as part of the entrepreneurship as a whole?
4. Which are the paragons that are involved drastically in SMEs' successful operation?

This chapter needs a specific focus because it is very crucial to be thoroughly understood in order to help us proceed with the rest of the book. For example, in order for students to understand the blue ocean strategy approach which is extremely important in terms of the entrepreneurial mentality that SME owners need to adapt, they need to understand in depth why this mentality is important in the first place. They also need to understand that running a small business needs to be considered as an integral part of entrepreneurship as a whole.

SECTION II

Financial Crisis and Small Business

CHAPTER 3

Implications of Financial Crisis in Small Business

Financial crisis and entrepreneurship. Financial crisis and small business. Management of risk paragons involved in small business. Active and passive enterprise risk management approach. The human capital risk. Credit risk. Bank lending and small business during financial crisis. Tax compliance. Small business company culture. The six components that drive cultural change.

3.1. Financial Crisis Impact on Small Business: The Example of the Last Global Financial Crisis

Financial stability can be beneficial to entrepreneurship in two ways (Wiebke and Winkler 2016). Firstly, according to Choi (1999, cited in Wiebke and Winkler 2016), it can be the springboard for entrepreneurship as economic transactions are governed to a high degree by the so-called conventional or normal behavior. Secondly, financial markets work properly during stability periods, something which allows entrepreneurs to be able to reach the opportunities they are seeking, which accordingly, as can be seen in Fogel et al. (2008, cited in Wiebke and Winkler 2016), enables the creation of a smooth process of "creative destruction" according to which while some economic agents create new routines, others adapt to them (Andersen, 2012:633, cited in Wiebke and Winkler 2016).

On the antipodes it can be said that the advent of financial crisis is a paragon which discourages entrepreneurship because it creates an environment in which uncertainty reaches high levels: something which worsens entrepreneurs' efforts toward the discovery of the opportunities they are seeking. Under this prism, entrepreneurs can be said that they tend to hesitate to take advantage of potential opportunities that arise under such circumstances, as the financial instability that financial crisis brings with it tends to erode the usual perception which says that what the entrepreneurial activity brings as its outcome is something which is largely determined not by the external paragons but mainly by the entrepreneur's actions, and thus decisions (Harper 2003, 91f, cited in Wiebke and Winkler 2016).

In addition, the sudden sharp reduction in credit availability during the financial crisis burdens entrepreneurial activities due to the lack of resources (Bernanke and Gertler 1989, cited in Wiebke and Winkler 2016). We all know how important it is for small businesses to secure their financing, especially during turbulent periods, so we can easily understand that reduction in credit availability can be fatal for small businesses.

It is clear from the above that financial crisis periods can create obstacles in entrepreneurial activities, which sometimes can be very difficult to overcome. Of course, many entrepreneurs might argue that crisis periods might lead to great opportunities, as during such periods markets are volatile and new businesses can arise, while many players might leave or new ones can come—situations that can alter the whole game. This is something which in combination with possible state regulations can be implemented by the government toward the alleviation of the companies' difficulties. Financing, for example, can be the great opportunity that many entrepreneurs seek in order to leverage the whole situation toward their company's development and growth.

But can we say that the last financial crisis of 2008 was a paragon which finally influenced small businesses negatively? Mills and McCarthy (2014), in their working paper about small business and their lending during the above-mentioned crisis in the United States, state that small companies were hit by the last global financial crisis harder than the larger ones, while the smallest were hit even hardest. They underscore that during the recession, between 2007 and 2012, small businesses in the United States lost about 60 percent of jobs, while payrolls at small businesses had a decrease of about 11 percent when at the same time the decrease in large corporations' payrolls was at about 7 percent (Mills and McCarthy 2014). It is impressive here to underline that jobs declined 14.1 percent in establishments which had less than 50 employees, while when there were 50 to 500 employees, the same number was at 9.5 percent and the overall employment number was even lower at about 8.4 percent (Mills and McCarthy 2014). It seems that the smaller the business, the smaller was the employment rate.

Kudlyak and Sánchez (2017), in one of their researches, also underline that small firms are negatively affected more than large firms during tight credit periods such as the one during the last global financial crisis of 2008. Not only that, they continue that the results of their research indicated that large firms' short-term debt and sales were decreased more than those of small firms during the last financial crisis and during the majority of the recession since the year 1969 (Kudlyak and Sánchez 2017).

Peric and Vitezic (2016), in a research they conducted based on a large number of companies that survived the big financial crisis of 2008 in both the manufacturing and the hospitality industry, using a two-step dynamic panel, found that turnover growth is positively correlated with the company's size during the period of time that the research was implemented (2008–2013). It was indicative that during this period of the big recession, the large and the medium firms presented higher growth rates than the ones that the small companies had (Peric and Vitezic 2016). It is obvious that in this case, size does count.

Based on surveys that were conducted during the global financial crises (2008 and 2009) in Japan by RIETI,[1] Ogawa and Takanori (2013) examined in their paper titled "The Global Financial Crisis and Small- and Medium-Sized Enterprises in Japan: How did they Cope with the Crisis?" how SMEs in Japan responded to the shocks that were caused by the big financial crisis waves that hit the country. The authors argue that these shock waves that hit Japan's SMEs were demand, supply, and financial shocks (Ogawa and Takanori 2013). From the above-mentioned shocks, the demand one was the strongest, while the financial one was the least frequent (Ogawa and Takanori 2013). The pattern that they observed was that SMEs in order to overcome these shocks, and especially the demand one, adapted several measures by trying to get the help they needed via their suppliers and the financial institutions with which they had an affiliation (Ogawa and Takanori 2013).

---

[1] RIETI: Research Institute of Economy, Trade and Industry is a policy think tank which was established during 2001 in Japan. Its mission is to implement public policy studies and analyses in order to be able to make policy proposals based on the results of such studies (Research Institute of Economy, Trade and Industry n.d.).

It is clear that the last big global financial crisis which had a vast impact on companies worldwide, when it came to SMEs, hit them very hard. Small businesses had more difficult time to survive and reorganize their core business, something which was depicted in the almost immediate decrease of their employment rate as we saw in the previous paragraphs. SMEs had a difficult time to survive, but when the state was able to help them via several methods, this struggle was successful. There were times, like in the Greek case, when financing from banks was almost zero and especially during the period when capital controls were enforced in the Greek market. Under such circumstances many thousands of SMEs were inevitably bankrupted as the combination of capital controls and almost zero bank financing was an extremely toxic one.

Small businesses can use financial crisis periods as a springboard for success by using disruptive approaches as we will see in a later chapter, but in general they face many problems, larger than the ones that bigger companies might face as well. So, although such periods can be an opportunity, they usually are dark periods for SMEs, especially for the ones which are facing financial problems or entering the crisis period with big financial burdens.

3.2   Management of Risk Paragons Involved

Risking in business is something that no company can avoid. All entrepreneurs know that from the very moment that they decide to start their business they should be prepared to take a risk. In fact the very event of beginning a new company is a risk of its own. The entrepreneurial mind-set is a mind-set which has made peace with risk. It is a nonrisk-averse mind-set, as it is clear to all real entrepreneurs that in order to establish their business in the long run, they need to risk, usually more than once during their company's life cycle.

In SMEs things are not different. SMEs, as a special company category, face special risks. For example, liquidity risks. It is imperative that SMEs' owners should be able to deal effectively with all the risks that are involved in their business. During financial crisis periods, risks might be bigger and decision making might be even more difficult as constraints and pressure are usually higher. This makes it very important for small business owners to adapt all the risk management mechanisms that are necessary in order to help them sustain and take the right decisions in due time.

But what is risk? Although everybody is quite familiar with the term, it is quite a controversial one. According to Aven (2012, cited in Karaoulanis 2017), risk has three possible definitions, which are the following:

1. Possibility of probable exposure to loss, damage, injury, or to other negative circumstances.
2. A hazardous journey, or a course of action or venture.
3. A person or a thing that could be regarded as a probable source of threat or danger (Aven 2012, cited in Karaoulanis 2017).

Now that we have got an idea of what risk is, we are going to see how risk is being perceived in SMEs and how they try to confront it. According to Brustbauer (2016), SMEs have the option to follow an active or a passive enterprise risk management (ERM)[2] approach, something which accordingly will affect their strategic planning and thus orientation.

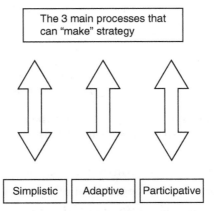

Figure 3.1 *The two approaches of risk management and their results in terms of the strategic approach that will be followed (Brustbauer 2016)*

---

[2]ERM: Enterprise risk management (ERM) is the process of planning, organizing, leading, and controlling all the activities involved in an organization in order to be able to minimize the effects of risk on the organization's capital and of course on profit. It involves risks that are correlated to financial, strategic, and operational aspects, in addition to risks associated with accidental losses (Brustbauer 2016).

Brustbauer (2016) also stresses that implementing the right ERM is crucial for SMEs, as it can be a factor which can be considered very powerful in terms of helping SMEs adjust to the continuous changing global environment, and via this adaptation help them gain their strategic competitive advantage which is crucial also in order to guide them toward the achievement of their so important sustainable development, and thus growth. Brustbauer (2016) continues that the paragons that are responsible and affecting the right implementation of the ERM are the size of the firm, the market sector affiliation, and finally the structure influence paragon.

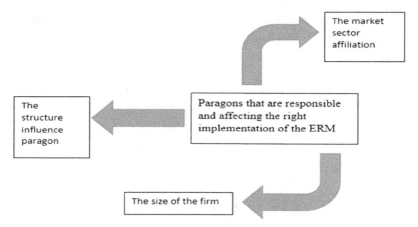

Figure 3.2 Paragons that are responsible and affect the right implementation of the ERM (Brustbaouer 2016)

Being able to measure and manage the risks taken, in general, is a crucial paragon for SMEs. As, especially during crisis years, they need to adapt to an ever-changing environment, they need to be able to understand the risks that they need to take. They also need to manage such risks in order to reduce them as much as they can and to be able to overcome the negative waves that might arise in case risks cannot be handled. Finally, while they are operating in a turbulent environment, in order to survive, many times they need to take decisions that are crucial, disruptive, and will have vast impact on their business. If the right risk management mechanisms are in place, such decisions will be taken in a more risk-minimized way and small businesses would be able to take their next step toward their future in a more safe and proper way. This is why risk management is so important, especially for SMEs during crisis years.

But although we can now understand what we are talking about when we are referring to SMEs' risks, we need to be more specific in terms of the risks they are facing. In the following paragraphs we will try to describe some of the most important risks that play a crucial role in the small company's operation as a whole, especially during turbulent times.

A risk that can play an important role in SMEs' growth is the human capital risk. Mäenpää and Voutilainen (2012) stress that insurance can play a vital role in terms of the management of human capital risks.[3] Human capital risks can be divided into two major categories, the insurable and the uninsurable risks (Mäenpää and Voutilainen 2012). Mäenpää and Voutilainen (2012) also conclude that the insurance types that are useful in a SME context of the company's human capital risk management are pension, accident, health, life, liability, and crime insurances. Having healthy employees and a clear state of mind regarding liabilities and crime is something which adds value to all small businesses as it helps them operate in a safer way and to produce in a better way as employees' well-being can be a decisive paragon which determines in high levels their productivity.

Gaul (2013) processes the importance of human capital risk management from another point of view. He argues that human capital risk can be defined as the very gap between the company's goals and its workforce skills. The importance of this fact per se is enormous, especially in the context of SMEs.

Organizations and especially SMEs which have a limited number of employees depend on groups of employees, which all contribute to the company's growth via their interaction in their specific division of labor (Gaul 2013). As this whole environment is quite complicated, employees may introduce several risks whether they want to or not. The result is that such risks, if they are not prevented by the company, are able to impose significant loses in the company's brand, reputation, morale, and of course revenue, thus profit (Gaul 2013).

---

[3]Human capital risk management: Is the leverage of human resource assets in order to achieve the organization's strategic and operational goals (Beyer 2015).

From the above, we can easily understand how important it is, especially for SMEs, to be able to handle in some way this human capital risk via a management procedure. Humans are the cornerstone of each small business. They are the main pillar upon which the whole company is being built. Small businesses, by nature, are establishing an intimate, in a way, bond between the owner and her employees. As SMEs usually have a local character, this bond has even large social implications. This is something which underlines the importance of human capital in terms of SMEs' evolvement and growth, especially as an integral part of the companies in question—corporate social responsibility actions. The way that SMEs are reaching society in terms of people's well-being is very unique. This is something that SMEs need to keep in mind as it is extremely valuable due to the bond that is created with its customers who usually are members of the local society where SMEs are operating.

There should be an equilibrium between human capital potential and knowledge and what is needed in terms of making the company operating in its maximum possible potential toward revenue. Also, risks that involve the human capital and might be crucial for the whole SME operations need to be treated in a discreet and delicate way because, as we said, several social and even personal implications, especially when SMEs have a local character, might arise. SMEs need to be able to manage such risks in an effective and delicate way.

Another important expression of risk in SMEs' life is the commercial processes risk. Žigienė et al. (2019) underline that risk management in commercial processes is one of the most important factors that can affect SMEs negatively in terms of their competitiveness, innovativeness, and potential contribution to the global sustainable development goals (SDGs). Žigienė et al. (2019) also argue that SMEs in order to be able to manage better all paragons involved in commercial risks could implement elements of artificial intelligence (AI), big data, and machine learning. Of course this kind of new technologies demands quite a high budget but in case groups of SMEs utilize them, it can be something that can be proved affordable for them (Žigienė et al. 2019).

It is the author's prevalent opinion that SMEs are quite difficult to be able to deploy A.I., big data, and machine learning projects in order to be able to predict future consumerist behaviors based on past trends, etc. This is quite difficult because, as we said above, SMEs usually have a tight budget, especially during financially turbulent periods. Generally speaking, the advent of A.I. in the next years will create two kinds of companies globally, ones that will be able to use A.I. in their core business as they will have the needed budget, and the ones that will not be able to use high-tech solutions like A.I. or machine learning as they will not have the needed budget.

As SMEs mostly belong to the second category, it will be imperative for them to be based mostly upon their personnel. The human factor will make the difference for them and will be their competitive advantage. Soft skills will be the ones that will differentiate their business from the ones that will implement A.I. in the decision process, etc. This is why the risk management of the human capital is extremely important and this is also why SMEs need to invest in their human capital in a more productive way. We need to understand that SMEs need to have in the epicenter of their business two major paragons: their human resources and their customers. Managing the risks that these two paragons might have is a very important factor in terms of their operations.

Credit risk is another risk that is extremely important for SMEs all over the globe, as it has to do with one of their major problems, financing. SMEs need to have access to finance in order to survive. Banks need to access SMEs' credit risks in order to be able to evaluate their position and to proceed with their lending. Belas et al. (2018) stress that in order for SMEs' credit risks to be managed effectively they need to be based on noneconomic factors, with the most important among them, the education and the family environment (Belas et al. 2018). Of course, economic factors can also be proved quite important in terms of the SMEs' relationship with the banking sector, not to mention that the need for financial knowledge in the area of capital and payment discipline is very important too (Belas et al. 2018).

Although the credit risk that small businesses are facing is extremely important in terms of their evaluation from the banking system toward their financing, it is not always that simple or easy. According to a white paper disseminated by Moody's (2016), the difficulties that banks face in order to address SMEs' credit risk have their root cause in fragmented financial data, the strength of risk models implemented, the length of the whole evaluation process, the tension between sales and credit, the competitiveness of the lending environment in which SMEs need to survive, the differentiation in geographies, the positions in the economics and credit cycles, etc. (Moody's 2016).

It is imperative for small businesses to maintain a good credit risk profile in order to be able to have access to banking financing. In order to achieve that they need somehow to be able to control their risk and especially the ones that are correlated with their liquidity. SMEs in order to be able to access all kinds of risks that they are facing during their life cycle need to implement risk management mechanisms. According to a Karaoulanis' (2017) research on SMEs in Greece during the last global financial crisis which had vast impact in the Greek economy and accordingly to the Greek society, although SMEs use some kind of risk management mechanisms, these are mainly informal.

This fact per se can be translated in multiple ways. SMEs especially during crisis years have no or little access to funding, something which makes it very difficult for them to implement sophisticated and expensive risk management mechanisms. Another translation could be that SME owners are aware of the potential risks and this is why they try to protect their companies via even informal risk management mechanisms of any possible and affordable kind. On the other hand, we need to say that sometimes the SMEs' owners, especially in micro-SMEs, believe in their experience and don't even use any kind of risk management mechanisms in order to take their decisions, something that can have devastating results in the short and in the long run (Karaoulanis 2017).

Also, there is a whole "different category" of SMEs, which is SMEs owned by one person. These are small businesses in which the owner and operator are the only persons that work for this company. Such companies can be seen all around us every day, everywhere. They are the small business in our neighborhood, like the grocery, etc. In such cases, although the owners are aware of the risks that are being faced on a daily basis, they usually are not people with a college background who are familiar with sophisticated methods or with cutting-edge tools. This is why they implement, sometimes even without realizing it, their risk management mechanisms which are simple but usually quite effective. For example, they have informal ways to check their inventory of goods, to forecast the market's next steps based on their "gut feeling," etc. Of course, there are several paradigms for the opposite, in other words, of one person-owned small business which didn't make it, sometimes because of the lack of risk management mechanisms which led to bad decisions.

On the same wavelength, Gao et al. (2013), in a research they conducted in an SME in China, stress that risk management mechanisms in SMEs usually have the form of informal processes and that the role of cognitive capital[4] is extremely important in the context of developing the right risk management mechanisms. They finally argue that cognitive capital is very important in accumulating structural[5] and relational[6] capital (Gao et al. 2013).

It is inevitable that SMEs will face some risks during their life cycle. Having the right risk management mechanisms in place is something that can be the crucial factor that will be able to save SMEs, especially during difficult periods of crisis. Although it is quite understandable that usually SMEs don't have the luxury of financing such mechanisms and that because of it they usually come up with informal mechanisms of risk control, it is imperative that SMEs need to have as a vital part of their operations some kind of risk management mechanisms that are appropriate for their business needs. Although sometimes SMEs are companies with just one person, they need to understand that running such companies needs to have as a prerequisite the right risk management mechanisms to be in place from the beginning, especially when we are talking about companies which started their operation during turbulent periods of time.

---

[4]Cognitive capital: "concept that represents knowledge as a scarce resource that can be traded with money, social influence, and political power. This concept is derived from Pierre Bourdieu's concept of 'cultural capital,' and it sheds light on accumulation and exchange processes regarding cognitive skills, knowledge, and information. Cognitive capital is now recognized as a key asset of institutions and economic organizations" (igi–global.com n.d.a).

[5]Structural capital: "Structural capital is the set of procedures, processes, and internal structures that contribute to the implementation of the objectives of an organization" (igi–global.com n.d.b).

[6]Relational capital: "It is the product of shared knowledge when it is effectively incorporated into an organization" (igi–global.com, n.d.c).

According to the New South Wales (NSW) Department of State and Regional Development (2005, cited in Karaoulanis 2017), there are three main types of risk which can be managed as follows:

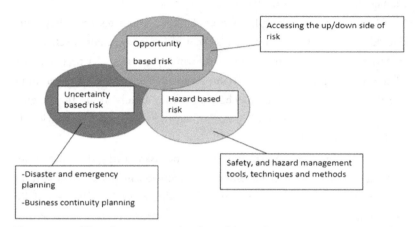

Figure 3.3 The three types of risk and how they are managed (NSW Department of State and Regional Development 2005, cited in Karaoulanis 2017)

Hubbard (2009, cited in Karaoulanis 2017) states that there are specific levels that can describe the implementation of the risk management mechanisms in SMEs in terms of their success or failure, which are the following (Table 3.1):

Table 3.1 The five levels of use of risk management mechanisms (Hubbard 2009, cited in Karaoulanis 2017)

BEST
BETTER
BASELINE
WORSE
WORST

1. **BEST:** When a company operates in that level, in order to confront its potential risk, it builds quantitative models which it uses

accordingly to run simulations with which the use of the appropriate risk management mechanisms and the statistical methods proven to help in that situation can validate all the inputs to check the results against the reality in a skeptical way. In that way the company in question is able to identify all the risks that might arise, before they will appear in order to confront them successfully (Hubbard 2009, cited in Karaoulanis 2017).

2. **BETTER:** In this level the SMEs' managers/owners probably build the quantitative models that are needed using at least some proven components. In that way the general scope of risk management expands in order to be able to include more of the risks (Hubbard 2009, cited in Karaoulanis 2017).

3. **BASELINE:** This is the level where we do not find any kind of formal risk management mechanisms in the SMEs in question. In such cases, managers use their intuition in order to access the risks and to implement the right strategies that are available and that will be able to mitigate the risks in question (Hubbard 2009, cited in Karaoulanis 2017).

4. **WORSE:** In that level, the methods that managers use are known as "soft" or "scoring" ones. Such methods can even be misapplied quantitative methods. This is a level that can be characterized as equally bad with the previous one, while some argue that companies that are categorized in that level can spend even more money and time than the ones of the previous level (Hubbard 2009, cited in Karaoulanis 2017).

5. **WORST:** In that level we can find SMEs that use ineffective methods but have great confidence in what they are doing, although such methods usually add error to their risk evaluation. The problem with such methods is that although they can be quite sophisticated and one could expected, and accurate too, in fact they can be quite erroneous and can lead to wrong decisions, that, Hubbard (2009, cited in Karaoulanis 2017) states, such mistakes "would have been avoided if no method at all have been used" (Hubbard 2009, cited in Karaoulanis 2017).

According to the research conducted by Karaoulanis (2017), in Greece, the main risk management mechanisms that SMEs usually use are the following:

1. Insurance
2. Liquidity management
3. Cash management
4. Safety and hazard management tools
5. Supply management
6. Stock management mechanisms
7. Risk assessment for reaching new opportunities (Karaoulanis 2017)

Almost all of the above-mentioned mechanisms that were examined during this specific research were informal ones. In other words, the specific SMEs, which we need to underline that they were operating in a turbulent environment under the shadow of that imposed by the Greek government capital controls and during the worst financial crisis the country ever faced, were operating from levels three to five under the Hubbard (2009, cited in Karaoulanis 2017) scale. This is indicative of the problem, which in a way can be described as a vicious cycle. SMEs need to confront their risks due to the ongoing crisis, but as they cannot be financed, they cannot afford sophisticated risk management techniques and methods and this is why they use informal ones. This results in increased risks that decrease the company's performance and results, something which makes things difficult, especially from a financial approach and lets them continue using their informal mechanisms as they continue to not be able to afford the sophisticated ones that will probably make a difference. Stranded in this vortex, small business owners feel helpless sometimes and all they want to do is to survive somehow; a mentality which increases their company's pathogenesis as it is amalgamated with severe lack of many paragons that are important, like the right company culture, education of personnel, risk management mechanisms, etc.

Generally speaking, using the right risk management mechanisms is something that SMEs' owners need to reconsider. Although it is something that in the eyes of many might be seen as a luxury, especially during turbulent years, in fact it is a crucial paragon that can help SMEs overcome the probable pitfalls that they might encounter and it can give them the competitive advantage they need in order to survive and sustain their business in the long run.

3.3 Bank Lending and Small Business during Financial Crisis

As we saw in previous paragraphs, liquidity is the number one problem that SMEs are facing, especially during crisis periods. The main factor that has vast impact in that paragon is bank lending as it can be considered as the number one source of financing for SMEs globally.

According to Daisuke (2015), who investigated the correlation between bank loan availability and trade credit for small businesses in Japan during the years of the last big global financial crisis, small businesses increased their trade credit, not only their payables but their receivables as well, when bank loan availability improved, something which results in the conclusion that there is a positive relationship between trade payables and bank loans for small business, not to mention that when small businesses have an enhanced credit availability they can offer a better trade credit to their customers as well (Daisuke 2015).

Deyoung et al. (2015) underline, in their U.S.-based research, that small businesses are very dependable in bank finance, while during financial crisis years the lack of such finance due to several reasons, like declining loan quality from the banks' part etc., credit can become less available, something which creates economic downturns to job-creating small business (Deyoung et al. 2015). The last global financial crisis and the ensuing recession found that the U.S. banks' lending to small businesses fell quite low (Kiser, Prager, and Scott 2016), something which of course affected to a high extent the timely recovery of such businesses which, as we know, are responsible for a big portion of new job creation (Kiser, Prager, and Scott 2016).

But although bank lending is extremely important to all kinds of SMEs on a global level, getting a bank loan is not something that simple for SME owners, especially during financial crisis years or when SMEs have a negative credit record. Many paragons can be involved, like the availability and the cost of the bank loans as such businesses often lack any other external sources of such financing (Berger and Udell 1998; Carbó-Valverde et al. 2009, cited in Sääskilahti 2016). It is very important here to underline that when uncertainty is at high levels and especially during financial crisis years, such bank financing to opaque small businesses largely declines (ECB 2014, cited in Sääskilahti 2016).

A question that many academics and researchers tried to answer in the recent years is the best way of banking financing of small businesses, especially during financial crisis years. Getting a loan from a small or a big bank?

According to a recent paper of Berger, Cerqueiro and Penas (2015), titled "Market Size Structure and Small Business Lending: Are Crisis Times Different from Normal Times?", small banks' lending to small business might have specific competitive advantages compared against big banks' lending to this category of businesses (Stein 2002, cited in Berger, Cerqueiro, and Penas 2015). Such advantages might be the fact that in small banks qualitative information can easily be gathered through relationships, something which is quite difficult in large banks which have multiple and sometimes impersonal communication channels to serve them toward that direction (Stein 2002, cited in Berger, Cerqueiro, and Penas 2015).

Another major problem for larger banks might be that they are "moving" slowly due to the many layers of approval which consist of the whole lending procedure, something which of course makes them less agile, as the qualitative relationship-based information can be more easily communicated throughout the bank's levels of approval as it seems is the case with the small ones (Berger and Udell 2002; Liberty and Mian 2009, cited in Berger, Cerqueiro, and Penas 2015).

Another problem that large banks might face is that they might suffer from so-called organizational diseconomies of scale[7] (Williamson 1988,

---

[7]Diseconomies of scale: Diseconomies of scale occur when increase in production output is accompanied with increase in marginal costs, something which finally results in a profitability decrease. In a way, it can be seen as the opposite of the economy of scale which is when the decrease in production costs is the result of the increase of the production output (Corporate finance institute n.d.).

cited in Berger, Cerqueiro, and Penas 2015), which have to do with the lending of large, more transparent companies based on quantitative information and with the delivering of loans to small and more opaque companies based on qualitative relationship-based information (Williamson 1988, cited in Berger, Cerqueiro, and Penas 2015). A recent approach indicates though that large banks can serve better than the small ones a portion of small business by providing loans that are based on quantitative data/information (Berger and Udell 2006, cited in Berger, Cerqueiro, and Penas 2015).

An important paragon that can influence the bank's lending to SMEs is the risk level at which they are exposed and the amount of delinquencies that they might have. A very interesting outcome has emerged as the result of a large-scale survey that was conducted in over 30,000 UK-based SMEs by Cowling Marc, Weixi Liu, and Ning Zhang (2016). The researchers found that, first of all, older firms and firms which had higher risk rating and a record of some kind of financial delinquency and were more likely to seek some kind of external (banking, etc.) finance. In addition, they also found that older firms, which were healthy enough without any delinquencies or high-risk rates, had an easier access to external financing, while banks were more or less unwilling to lend to companies which were at the high-risk region or had a past history of delinquencies of some kind (Cowling, Weixi and Zhang 2016).

Carbó-Valverde et al. (2016), in their paper titled "Trade Credit, the Financial Crisis, and SME Access to Finance," conducted a research using firm-level Spanish data in which they found that during the large global financial crisis, SMEs which were credit constrained tend to depend on trade credit and not on bank lending, while, on the other hand, credit unconstrained firms were mostly depended on bank loans and not on trade credit (Carbó-Valverde et al. 2016).

From the above, we can understand that especially during financial crisis years, SMEs face several problems in terms of their external financing, especially when it comes from the banking sector. So, since SMEs during such years have to deal with this liquidity shortage which springs for the "unwilling" banks' behavior to lend them, they have to turn to alternative sources of financing their business. Under this prism, many

SMEs turn to what is called trade credit[8] in order to be able to secure the smoothly operational run. In Greece, for example, there is a trade credit approach to money checks. Business owners, as part of their bargain with their suppliers, can give them a money check which might be payable even after six months or so. In that way they can have their merchandise, while all they give to their suppliers is in fact a promise that they will pay them after six months or so. This is something that is the norm at least the last 20 to 25 years in Greece. Things changed quite a lot during the last financial years, as suppliers started to get this kind of money checks only from clients that they trusted as there was a domino of companies that suddenly went bankrupt without paying their obligations.

3.4   Tax Compliance

Every individual and every company needs to operate in a safe environment in order to thrive and grow. Such environments can only be provided by the state in which they operate as its integral part. Operating in a stable environment which can be translated into a stable government and stable long-term laws regarding taxes, trade and operational procedures, is vital for all companies and of course for SMEs, not only regarding how they need to approach their daily operations, but also in terms of their future plans and strategies. Tax compliance is a very important factor which has many implications for all businesses and need to be addressed under the prism of tax laws, stability, and governmental trustworthiness.

According to SARS (2012, cited in Bornman and Stack 2015), tax compliance can be described as "the degree to which taxpayers and traders along with intermediates like practitioners and clearing agents meet their legal obligations" (SARS 2012, cited in Bornman and Stack 2015:792).

According to Smulders and Naidoo (2013), small businesses are crucial for the society as a whole and of course for the economy as they have

---

[8]Trade credit: According to Entrepreneur.com (n.d.), "For many businesses, trade credit is an essential tool for financing growth. Trade credit is the credit extended to you by suppliers who let you buy now and pay later. Any time you take delivery of materials, equipment or other valuables without paying cash on the spot, you're using trade credit."

the potential to intervene in a very constructive way as they can grow economy, generate new job positions, and alleviate poverty, something which is extremely important. Toward that direction, they face several impediments like financing and high tax compliance costs and burdens (Smulders and Naidoo 2013). So, tax compliance problems can be proved quite important for the SMEs' overall operation as we will be able to analyze in the following paragraphs.

Lynley Woodward and Lin Mei Tan (2015) conducted a research regarding small business owners (SBO) in New Zealand tax compliance attitude. Their research was focused in SBOs' perception of chance to be audited and/or penalized, their tax morale, the social norms that depict other business tax payers' compliance behavior, their tax system perception in terms of its fairness, tax burden, etc. and their trust to the authority which imposes these taxes (Woodward and Tan 2015).

The results of their research indicated that:

1. Many SBOs perceive the tax system as quite complicated and not easy to follow.
2. Many SBOs mainly rely on specific accounting software in order to record the taxable transactions, while assuming that tax practitioners would find out potential mistakes.
3. The SBOs had tax audits and fines that might be posed to consider.
4. The majority of SBOs tried to file a correct and timely tax return in fear of an eminent risk of incurring penalties as a result of not doing so.
5. The SBO's morale with regard to both proper invoicing and classification of goods and services was positive, although some of them suspected a few of not following legal rules by falsifying invoices and classifications.
6. Many of the SBOs that participated in the research were familiar with the customers' preference to pay in cash in order to avoid paying taxes and, something that was quite impressive and revealing, about one-third of the SBOs that were questioned admitted that they did the same themselves!

(Woodward and Tan 2015).

Swistak (2016), in his paper titled "Tax Penalties in SME Tax Compliance," underlined that small business tax compliance is a factor that need not be taken lightly and which needs special attention. This is because small businesses are often in a difficult position in terms of paying their tax obligations, they are exposed to a greater degree to external risks, and because of their potential liquidity problems, they are tempted to not fulfill their tax obligations (Swistak 2016). He continues that toward that direction what differentiates them from larger businesses is that small businesses are usually owner-operated, something which means that they are highly responsive to personal, social, cognitive, and emotional factors which are involved in their decision-making process (Swistak 2016). In simple words, SMEs having their owners as the ones responsible for the decision making in terms of the company's tax compliance are more vulnerable in decisions that are influenced by many paragons which lie outside the business spectrum and interfere more with their owner's social acquaintances or family, which are paragons that influence their decisions.

In a recent research conducted by Battisti and Deakins (2018), who used grounded theory and conducted in-depth interviews with 42 SBOs who were matched with their firms' factual tax compliance status, the results indicated that high capability does not necessarily translate into high tax compliance, while this kind of relationship between these two factors is mediated mainly by the managers-owners' perception regarding taxation in their surrounding economic and regulatory environment (Battisti and Deakins 2018).

What is important to underline here is that tax compliance for SMEs during financial crisis years is a paragon which although sometimes tend to be underestimated by some, in fact, is crucial. SME owners in order to gain some time to pay their obligations, as they do not have the luxury to be financed, can be tempted to not fulfill their legal tax obligations. For example, they might be tempted to tell their customers to not give them a receipt for the goods they just bought and thereby to sell it to them at a lower price. Although such behavior reduces the state's revenue from taxation, for the SMEs in question it can prove vital as it will help them cover some of their obligations in the short run. For some it is all about survival, while for others it is all about finding the right opportunity to steal.

It is clear enough that as SMEs are the big majority of all businesses in every society, tax compliance issues might create huge problems for the state and its income from taxation. This accordingly might result in new rules imposed by the state tax laws that will be harder than the old ones, something which will also increase the SME owners' temptation to not be tax compliant. It will create, in other words, another vicious cycle, which in the long run will have vast social implications on everybody as it will probably affect even the prices of the goods or the citizens' taxation. This fact per se is indicative of the importance of tax compliance for SMEs and is ringing a bell to all authorities and people involved in the case to act drastically toward the right direction, especially during crisis years when SMEs try hard to survive and solve their liquidity problems. In that direction, the state should impose the right laws regarding heavy SMEs' taxation in order to help them relieve from their financial burdens and strengthen their position. The results toward that direction will be extremely valuable and will have a very positive societal impact.

It is important here to also underline that as we saw in the previous paragraphs, small business owners sometimes might be tempted not to be compliant with their tax obligations, especially during financially turbulent periods of time when they might face huge liquidity problems. Although this might seem like a good solution at the moment, it might impose high fees to the small business in question, something which in combination with its liquidity problems can bring it to the verge of seizing its operations. So tax compliance has a dual impact to small businesses during financial crisis periods, one which has negative results to the society as a whole and another which can affect very negatively the business itself.

3.5   Small Business Company Culture

Company culture is an extremely important factor in business in general and in small business as well. It can be the decisive paragon that will help employees feel better and fulfilled, something which will make them grow professionally and personally and, in accordance, will benefit business in multiple ways as it will help them in being more productive. As Peter Drucker once said, "culture eats strategy for breakfast," something which underlines its importance, which is above even the overall company strategy.

For SMEs adapting a great company culture is, as we will see in the paragraphs to follow, a very important factor upon which they need to build their own future as it can be used as the strongest pillar of their growth and sustainable development.

According to Levine (2018), research has shown that the implementation of the right work culture is responsible for having employees inspired while working, something which helps to a great degree in increasing the company's fiscal performance. On the contrary, Levine (2018) underlines that a toxic working environment will decrease motivation and inspiration—something which sooner or later will be depicted in the company's decrease in profits.

Levine (2018) indicates the six ways/components that are necessary in order to help any kind of business to change its company culture in a positive way that will help employees and boost performance and thus profits. These six components are depicted in Table 3.2.

Table 3.2 The six components that drive cultural change in business (Levine 2018)

Purpose	It is the major component that both inspires and guides.
Values	It is a powerful component as well which helps in establishing the behavioral expectations of both leaders and employees.
Behaviors	These can be described as the "culturally aligned symptoms and actions of a work culture" (Levine 2018).
Recognition	It's a way of reward in a very effective way.
Rituals	These can be described as the regular activities that help in building a strong bond/relationship between employees and leaders.
Cues	They are physical and behavioral ways of reminding everyone in the company of the company's purpose and goals for the future.

Another important fact, especially in the last few years, is that employees regularly suffer from mental health issues that are correlated to their working environment. Such issues can be very costly in the long run not only for business but for the state itself too. According to Sime (2019), on a global scale, more than 300 million people suffer from depression. This, as the author concludes, leads to an estimated $1 trillion each year in lost productivity. The number is huge and it increases year by year.

Mental health is extremely important for all businesses and of course for the small ones. It can help employees achieve good results, while at the same time can help them achieve a life–work balance during their off time (My-e-health.se n.d.). This will have a positive impact on their work performance, something which in the long run will help them achieve the company goals better. Especially during crisis years when stressful situations are more frequent, such results are in higher demand by SBOs and can help them achieve their sustainable development targets which will help them get out from the difficult situations they are facing. Making changes in the already embedded company culture which will be able to improve employees' mental health, and thus well-being and performance, is not something which is costly and can be implemented by small business easily. All they need is for their owners to have the appropriate mentality which will help them understand the importance of the issue, something which will be possible to motivate them toward such changes (Table 3.3).

Table 3.3 Five small changes that cost a minimal amount but are thought to improve an employee's well-being considerably (Mind foundation n.d., cited in Sime 2019)

1. Enforce working hours.
2. Avoid employees working in a solely isolated way.
3. Set achievable deadlines and spread workloads equally and fairly across employees and teams.
4. Provide support services and staff members who have had training in mental health and workplace stress.
5. Promote healthy eating and regular exercise.

It is absolutely imperative for small businesses, and businesses in general, to promote a great company culture in their workplaces, which will help employees be improved as human beings not only in terms of their work performance and personality as a whole but also in terms of their mental health. When times are turbulent and hard work under stressful conditions is required to lead to high results, such culture will help the small business in question to thrive as its employees will be able to perform better than others who need to work in worst working environments, something which will be the company's competitive advantage and will help it grow, even during the most difficult circumstances.

But great company culture is not only a very important paragon in terms of boosting performance and increasing profits. It is also a very strong weapon in the management's hands which helps the company to prevent crime and promote integrity as Bussmann and Niemeczek (2019) stress via a research they conducted on about 2,000 managers in German parent companies and about 600 managers in Central and North European branch offices. So, in a way, it can be seen as a matter of perspective. It is better to be proactive by cultivating the right ethical standards in the company's culture instead of trying to solve problems when they arise, especially ethical and integrity ones.

In a similar research that Bussmann and Niemeczek conducted one year earlier in 2018, they indicated that the implementation of the right company culture can also be preventive of the corruption on company level in general. This web-based research among 15 companies in Germany which all had an international profile resulted in underlining that the most important preventing factors in terms of corruption are a culture of integrity, a strong knowledge of the norms that the company uses in its daily tasks, and a high level of acceptance of the company's anticorruption program from the employees' part (Bussmann and Niemeczek 2018).

They stress that in order for such company culture to be implemented, the tone should come from the top. The direct superiors should be able to practice ethical leadership. and the general set of values that the company embraces should be conveyed via training in a way that employees will be able to understand how important such behavior is and that these values will help them very much in promoting their career (Bussmann and Niemeczek 2019). When it comes to SMEs, it is extremely important that the SME owner will have the right mentality in terms of the company culture that needed to be imposed.

Apart from helping employees' overall performance which contributes in the best possible way to the company's revenue and from assisting the implementation of a non-corruption climate in the company, the right company culture can also be extremely helpful in creating a positive reaction from the customers' part, something that can lead to many benefits like customer retention, word of mouth, revenue increase, etc. A very interesting approach on the company culture is the one which was deployed by Papke and Inc. Books24x7 (2013). According to this approach a critical factor in terms of how to achieve high customer satisfaction and via it, high customer retention, is what is called alignment. Alignment has to do with the ability any company has to communicate and deliver their services on the promise their brand makes to their customers (Papke and Inc. Books24x7 2013). In other words the company needs to deliver what it promises, otherwise it is going to lose its customers' loyalty and thus retention in the long run.

So, the given to the company's customers, services should be of the level and expectations the customers have due to the company's branding. In order for companies to achieve such alignment between what the company promises to offer and what it offers, it is crucial that leaders should define the company's vision and strategies that support the company's intentions, that is, on how to deliver the final product, etc., and such vision and mission should be communicated thoroughly in all company's levels (Papke and Inc. Books24x7 2013).

From the above, we can understand that not only SME owners need to implement a positive, customer-centric, and ethical company culture, but they need to communicate it to their employees in the right and effective way in order to help them align with the company's values, vision, and goals. This kind of communication usually is the responsibility of the managerial team, usually in a vertical way as it is disseminated from the top of the hierarchy toward the bottom. After the whole message is transmitted to the managerial personnel, the dissemination should be horizontal in order to reach everybody anywhere they work. Also, other "instruments" that can be used toward such communication and dissemination are meetings. During the meetings, managers will be able not only to disseminate what the top hierarchy wants the personnel to be aligned with in terms of the company culture, its vision, targets, and its customer-centric approach, but it would also be able to understand and correct possible mistakes or any other problems that might arise during that meeting.

In order for employees to be able to communicate the problems that they see via their daily interaction with the customers, the right culture needs to be implemented, a culture which will give employees the freedom to express their feelings and ideas without being afraid. This culture is the one which respects employees and makes them feel as an integral part of the team. Such an approach will not only be beneficial for any SME during financial crisis years, but it can be the springboard toward customer retention and growth. It can be the company's competitive advantage and it will cost absolutely nothing to the company in question.

Such an approach is extremely important in order to help companies of any size to decipher customers' expectations and help toward creating the icon that the specific brand is the answer to the customers' needs. So, it is obvious that creating a brand culture in which everybody that works for the company will be aligned with the company's mission and vision and is responsible for giving to the customers what the brand promised them to take is a major paragon in customer satisfaction which leads to customer retention, thus growth and increase in profits (Papke and Inc. Books24x7 2013).

We need to add here that the advent of technology the last few years couldn't be less than a vital part of the company's overall operation, and thus the company's culture. Medforth (2016) argues that although technology till now was not considered to be an important paragon that is involved in the implementation and evolvement of the company's culture, the changes that occurred during the last few years on the organizational level and especially the consumerization of IT in parallel with the increasing numbers of millennial workers in enterprise organizations, the quality performance, and the user experience of corporate IT led things in a way that technology has become an important player in morphing the company's culture (Medforth 2016).

Medforth (2016) argues that using technology and data in the right way can streamline business process, something which will eventually free up time and resources for the HR department. This, although it might seem trivial in the first place, it surely isn't as the HR department now can use its resources toward staff engagement and retention (Medforth 2016). It can be said then that in the years to come, the companies that focus on innovation and in progress in terms of technological trends to be followed will be the ones that will be able to have their employees happy via a great company culture and in that way they will be able to remain ahead of competition, as their competitive advantage will be their very employees (Medforth 2016).

From the above we can understand that company culture is one of the most important paragons that SMEs need to take into consideration for multiple reasons. Such reasons are that they can enhance the employees' productiveness, create high customer engagement and retention, create a climate inside the very company of high ethical standards and away from corruption, and can be combined with high technology and even A.I. in order to make employees more productive and happy. All these company culture results can be proved vital for small businesses especially during crisis periods as they can enhance productivity thus revenue and can create happy and most of all loyal customers, while the use of new technologies can be the catalyst toward great results. Such important elements can give to every SME the competitive advantage needed in order to overcome crisis and move toward its sustainable development.

Another important parameter in terms of company culture is training. It is very important for small businesses, especially during financially difficult periods of time, to embed in their company culture an employee's training program. In that way, the company's employees will be happier as they will be able to see that the company is caring for their development, and of course, they will be equipped for all major changes in their industry, a knowledge which can bring to the company in question better results via its employees' better performance.

In reality, employees' training programs in small business are facing many barriers. Pattanee Susomrith and Alan Coetzer (2015) in their research concluded that the main barriers such training is facing in small business workplaces are the following:

1. Due to the fact that in small businesses there are strong allocation norms which usually leave the training part outside, there is no proactive behavior regarding access to external training and development which is perceived as costly and not that important as other strategic parts.

2. What the research unveiled is that the main barriers that were observed came from within the company and not from the industry in general. So, mainly internal and not external factors are the problem.
3. There appears to be a significantly different approach between employees and SBOs regarding how they perceive employees' training and its barriers (Susomrith and Coetzer 2015).

On the same wavelength, Bai, Yuan and Pan (2017), in their research that took place in China between 533 SMEs, underline that SBOs are more concerned with their return on the firm's investment which springs from their employees' training, rather than their employees' benefits that spring from their very training.

In their research which sampled 448 family and 470 nonfamily SMEs that were separated into four size groups, Kotey and Folker (2007) found many interesting results. The results indicated that as the firm size was increasing in nonfamily small businesses, we had an increase in the formal, structured, and development-oriented employees' training. This phenomenon even increased more when it came to companies with a size between 20 and 99 employees. For family companies, formal training programs were increased during their critical growth phase which is estimated by the researchers with between 20 and 49 employees. The researchers conclude that the gaps that were observed between the family and the nonfamily small business were narrowed after the 100–199 employee limit. The results of the research in terms of the family-owned small businesses were pointed out to the correlation between the low formal training and the informal management styles, the limited financial resources, and the greater emphasis that this type of small business is giving to efficiency (Kotey and Folker 2007).

Family-owned small businesses seem to have their pathogenesis based inside their very heart of operations. In terms of employees' training it is imperative for their owners to change their mentality in terms of how they perceive their priorities against training. They need to understand that even when times are difficult, having well-trained employees who are working in a great company culture and feel themselves respected and well educated on all industry trends will bring to the company a return on investment much bigger than the monetary one. It will give them the competitive advantage they are seeking to let them get out of the financial vortex they are stranded into. They will be able to even apply innovation and blue ocean strategy tactics and be able to not only survive but also to start walking toward their sustainable development.

Author's Notes

In this chapter we deal with some of the most important factors that determine the small business' future during the financial crisis years.

Main points:
- First of all we need to understand that although a financial crisis can be the end for many small businesses due to several paragons like the lack of financing, it can also be a great opportunity to escape from the crisis and to grow via disruptive approaches like the blue ocean strategy which we will analyze further in the chapters to follow.
- Another important part of this chapter is the risk and its management. SMEs need to deal with their risk, especially during difficult periods. Almost all researches underlined that the majority of contemporary SMEs are not having formal or sophisticated risk management mechanisms. We also deal with the two approaches of risk management, the three main risk categories, and the risk levels.
- Finally, we underlined the importance of bank lending and we described several of its characteristics, while we stressed the importance of the SMEs' tax compliance and we noted how important it is for their overall performance and the SMEs' character.

Emphasis should be given to the risk management, the bank lending, the owners' entrepreneurial mentality, and the company culture. Especially the last one, which as we saw is in close relationship with technology. It can be argued that the advent of A.I. in the years to come will make it inevitable for SMEs which probably, at least at the beginning, will not be able to afford it, to use in the best possible way their human factor. As decisions and critical thinking are not what A.I. is capable of, the human factor can be crucial which will permit small businesses to compete with large ones which will be able to use A.I. and machine learning, etc. Company culture will be a catalyst toward that direction. This can be a great discussion topic in the class.

Suggested questions:
1. How can risk be defined? Why is risk management that important to small business?
2. How can company culture affect results of small businesses in the long and short run? Can company culture be combined with technology and how? Any suggestions?
3. How important is bank lending in terms of financing small business, especially during financial crisis periods?

CHAPTER 4

Small Business Entrepreneurial Strategic Approach during Financial Crisis

Small business investment strategies. Small business sustainable reorganization and turnaround management. Innovation strategy. Open innovation in small business.

4.1 Small Business Financing Sources and Impediments

As seen in previous chapters, financing small business is a crucial paragon regarding their sustainability. There are three main ways in which small business can be financed—get banking financing (loans), finance themselves with their own capitals, or get some private financing.

We all know that if the small business in question is a startup, private financing comes from specific sources like angel[1] investors and venture capitals (VCs).[2]

---

[1]Angel investors: They are private investors who are, of course, wealthy individuals who invest in a startup company or an entrepreneur with cash or capital in exchange of ownership or convertible debt because they believe in the company that it will succeed. They believe that the company will succeed (https://www.myaccountingcourse.com/ n.d.b).

[2]Venture Capital: A venture capitalist is a person or a company that invests in a business venture. They invest in capital to a startup to a company which wishes to expand. The majority of venture capitals come from professionally managed public or private firms. Their business is to pool investment funds from different sources and to invest in companies/business that are likely to give them high rates of return (Ward 2019).

Sudek (2006), trying to determine the main differences between how these two categories of financing operate, underlines that their main difference is that they follow a completely different process. He points out that VCs perform more due to diligence than angels. He refers to a recent study which found that 71 percent of VC's and only eight percent of angel investors take more than three references (Sudek 2006). Generally speaking, in terms of reference taken, VCs average four while on the other hand, angel investors only one (Van Osnabrugge 1998, cited in Sudek 2006).

As angel investors perform less due to lack of professional diligence, one can say that their investment approach seems more than an opportunistic one as it relies more on instincts while they tend not to calculate internal rates of return on investment etc. (Timmons 1990; Baty 1991; Mason and Harrison 1996; Van Osnabrugge and Robinson 2000, cited in Sudek 2006).

During crisis years small business and entrepreneurial orientations (SMEs) need to take action regarding the usual problem which is the self-financing one for any kind of investment which will help them grow and overcome their eminent financial and even operational problems. As liquidity is the number one enemy on such occasions, SMEs need to understand that they have to take some actions toward controlling it in the best possible way. The solutions that they have in hand are the banking loans, the funds that come from angel investors, the funds that come from VC, and their own financing. They need to take the right steps in one of these directions in order to be able to handle stressful situations that might arise and overcome potential financial pitfalls.

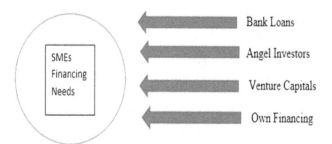

Figure 4.1 The main sources of financing SMEs

Koksal and Orgul (2007, cited in Ausloos et al. 2018) underlined that when SMEs face such problems during such crises, their first reaction usually is the implementation of cost saving policies, the interruption of any investment plans that they might have had in mind, and restructuring their business in a way that their goal is to cut costs. SMEs favor such actions due to the fact that usually such actions have some direct tangible results. On the other hand, such actions are impossible to secure the company's future (Koksal and Ozgul, 2007, cited in Ausloos et al. 2018).

Although the abovementioned approach of cutting costs, even if such costs involve the company's interruption of its investment plans, sounds reasonable enough for many small business entrepreneurs who struggle to make their business survive under severe liquidity problems, it is extremely questionable whether they will help the company in question toward its long-term survival.

Reeves and Deimler (2009, cited in Ausloos et al. 2018) argue that management's first move on such occasions should be to somehow secure the resources needed, especially liquidity. History has shown though that during financial crisis years the implementation of such defensive tactics has almost never driven SMEs into success in the long run (Reeves and Deimler, 2009, cited in Ausloos et al. 2018).

The research results of Ausloos et al. (2018) indicated that for SMEs, in order to be more resilient in the crisis in question, they need to start operations with lower assets. They continue that an extremely important point in terms of when investments should occur is the right timing (Ausloos et al. 2018). They argue that it is better for SMEs during recession years to adapt an increasing policy in terms of their investment rates instead of a decreasing one (Ausloos et al. 2018).

4.2 Turnaround Management during Turbulent Periods

When things are not going well, there aren't so many options. In fact, either you will persist and go on with the situation accepting it as it is, hoping that things will get better for some reason, or you will take the whole thing under consideration and try to change it in a way favorable to you. The second approach is guiding entrepreneurs to the notion of "turnaround management."

But what is turnaround management? According to Study.com (n.d.), turnaround management is the process followed when reviving the company in question while it is struggling to survive under usually difficult circumstances. Whether the company is facing financial problems or just competing against fierce competition in a saturated market, there may come a time when it needs to consider a turnaround management process as part of its strategic plan (Study.com n.d.).

According to H. Bhasin (2019), turnaround management follows five certain steps which are:

1. Define and analyze
2. Scope and strategy
3. Link and action
4. Implement
5. Review

But turnaround management is not a panacea and its implementation does not always mean that it will be a guaranteed success. Collett et al. (2014) conducted a research on a sample of 228 returns via a factor and logit[2] analysis method. They found four categories in terms of factors that led turnaround to a decline. They were the following:

1. Low quality management
2. High debt during adverse macro-economy
3. The very adverse microeconomic environment in which the companies had to operate
4. One-off causes of decline (Collett et al. 2014)

---

[2]Logit analysis or logistic analysis: A predictive analysis. "Logistic regression analysis is used to examine the association of (categorical or continuous) independent variable(s) with one dichotomous dependent variable" (Sciencedirect.com n.d.).

In addition, they underlined, as their research result, three main recovery action categories:

1. Management change and cash generation in addition
2. Reorientation in terms of the targeted markets in addition to cost-cutting
3. General company retrenchment (Collett et al. 2014)

Table 4.1 Factors that are important in successful and unsuccessful turnarounds (Collett et al. 2014)

Factors More Important in Successful Turnarounds	Factors More Important in Unsuccessful Turnarounds
One-off causes of decline	Poor management
Management change and cash generation	Adverse microeconomic environment
Cost-cutting and retrenchment	

Another crucial paragon that is involved heavily in the whole turnaround process is the stakeholders' presence and involvement. In a study conducted in Germany by Decker (2018), the results shown were that when stakeholders, in our case savings banks, provide SMEs with structural and continuing support they can assist them to a high degree with their turnaround process. It was found that such support, although conductive in the initial stage of turnaround, is negligible in the so-called recovery stage (Decker 2018).

Turnaround management is an important process that can help small businesses to change their operational scenery when times are difficult and proceed toward their reorganization and improvement of their business. It can help them acquire the competitive advantage that they are seeking.

A research conducted in Austria by Mayr, Mitter, and Aichmayr (2017) had as its epicenter SMEs' bankruptcy and how they can be overcome. As bankruptcy is one major negative problem that SMEs face on a global scale, Mayr, Mitter, and Aichmayr (2017) tried to uncover the factors that will help SMEs overcome bankruptcy. Using longitudinal data,[3]

---

[3]Longitudinal data: Refers to data which tracks the same sample at different points in time (Nlsinfo.org n.d.).

Mayr, Mitter, and Aichmayr (2017) were able to identify the most important factors which lead to sustainable reorganization of bankrupt SMEs
in Austria that were responsible for ensuring long-term survival and of
course, competitiveness. So, according to these results, a very important
factor which helps SMEs in their pivoting process is their repositioning,
which has as its main characteristic the paragon which gives SMEs their
competitive advantage and is their unique selling proposition combined
with innovation of some kind and the company's integration into networks (Mayr, Mitter, and Aichmayr 2017).

A very important part of the whole turnaround process is strategy. It
is quite interesting to take a glimpse how SMEs' administration mechanisms can help them introduce strategic change as part of their turnaround process.

Brunninge, Nordqvist, and Wiklund (2007) used a longitudinal
sample of 800 SMEs and found that closely held SMEs exhibit less strategic change than SMEs which rely on ownership structures that are
more widespread. Brunninge, Nordqvist, and Wiklund (2007) underline
though that SMEs which are more closely held can also achieve wide
strategic change if they will be able to use directors from outside or alter-
natively, by extending the size of the top management teams.

As stated in the beginning of this book, SMEs' survival is a crucial
socioeconomic factor, as their influence to societal prosperity is huge.
Mayr and Lixl (2019), in order to be able to analyze the root causes of
SMEs' crisis and how to proceed to successful restructuring towards their
survival, conducted multiple case studies in 10 successfully restructured
firms in Austria via the use of resource-based view (RBV)[4] in order to be
able to analyze the root causes of SMEs crisis and how to proceed to successful restructuring. Mayr and Lixl (2019) found that the main cause of
SMEs' crisis is predominantly rooted inside SMEs and that in order for
the restructuring to succeed, SMEs should engage both internal and external paragons that are involved, namely both the financing sources (i.e.,
banks) and the entrepreneurs.

---

[4]Resource-Based View (RBV): Is a model that sees resources as key to superior firm
performance. If a resource exhibits VRIO attributes, the resource enables the firm to
gain and sustain competitive advantage (Jurevicius 2013).

What is important here to underline is that SMEs' usual structure is the family one. This fact per se creates pros and cons. It creates a culture of trust and the company can be viable in the long run, as the successor of the CEO is ready and knows the job. Mayr and Lixl (2019) found that although innovation is quite critical as a factor in restructuring, complex and insufficiently settled family dynamics tend to create impediments toward SMEs' restructuring. So, what is obvious is that SMEs need to have the right managerial approach and that ownership and its dynamics can also play a vital role in the whole operation of the company, and thus its restructuring as well.

4.3   Innovation

Innovation[5] is a paragon which needs to be embedded in all businesses. As we will discuss in the next paragraphs, innovation is one of the major paragons that make business thrive, especially when things are difficult, e.g., when markets are saturated etc. Since sustainable development[6] is a critical paragon for SMEs, innovation needs to be considered as a crucial factor of that paragon.

Innovation can be found in several forms as we can see in the following. Klewitz and Hansen (2014) refer to "sustainability-oriented innovations" (SOIs)[7] as a factor which started the last years to be investigated in SMEs as well and not only in large firms as in the not distant past. The authors argue that this form of innovation has nowadays increasingly started to be recognized as the main component in SMEs' sustainable development (Klewitz and Hansen 2014). Klewitz and Hansen (2014) also argue that as the innovation process that SMEs are following is something that

---

[5]Innovation: According to Businessdictionary.com (n.d.), innovation is the process of translating an idea or an invention into a good or service which will be able to create value to the company's customers and for which they are willing to pay.

[6]Sustainable development: "Sustainable development is development that meets the needs of the present without compromising the ability of future generations to meet their own needs" (IISD n.d.).

[7]Sustainability-oriented innovations (SOIs): "the integration of ecological and social aspects into products, processes and organizational structures" (Klewitz and Hansen 2014).

changes over time, the interaction with external players such as customers, authorities, researchers, etc. can be crucial and can be held in order to help SMEs increase their innovative capacity for SOIs.

Another form of innovation which is very interesting for small businesses to consider is the so-called open innovation. According to Chesbrough, Vanhaverbeke, and West (2006), open innovation is when companies implement their research and development programs by using paragons that can be found outside their own company boundaries. They argue that in some cases, for example in the case of open software, this kind of research and development can take place in a nonproprietary way (Chesbrough, Vanhaverbeke, and West 2006). Sungjoo et al. (2010) in their research in Korean SMEs concluded that open innovation is a form of innovation that has a lot of potential in terms of being implemented in SMEs, while that potential can be facilitated via the right use of networking.

The importance of open innovation for SMEs, especially during difficult periods, is underlined also by Spithoven, Vanhaverbeke, and Roijakkers (2013). The authors indicate that the results of the implementation of open innovation in SMEs are different when used in large companies. SMEs usually face a lack of resources. This fact per se can be seen by someone as a barrier towards their extroversion efforts in their quest for knowledge which will help them acquire the competitive advantage their need. On the other hand, some can argue that this lack of resources is an opportunity for SMEs to be more extrovert towards their quest for technological knowledge (Spithoven, Vanhaverbeke, and Roijakkers 2013).

Innovation seems to be a very important component in SMEs' overall strategy toward sustainable development. In order for SMEs to leverage the healing results of innovation, they need to have embedded an innovation culture. Such culture can be strengthened by several ways, one of which, maybe the most important, is the collaboration with public research organizations (PROs) (Olmos-Peñuela et al. 2017).

In an empirical study based on a survey of SMEs collaborating with the largest Spanish PRO, the Spanish National Research Council (CSIC), Olmos-Peñuela et al. (2017) found that SMEs differ to a great degree in terms of how much they were able to strengthen their innovation culture via such collaborations.

Olmos-Peñuela et al. (2017) also conclude that SMEs which had formal innovation plans embedded in their overall company culture, and were able to develop internal and external search strategies were more likely to improve and extend their innovation culture as the result of this collaboration they had with PROs. The abovementioned research is indicative of the importance of SMEs' collaboration with such organizations toward their innovation plans and their long-term sustainable development, especially during crisis years which involves innovation as a very determining paragon of their core strategy and culture.

We understand that company culture refers to many things, from employees' well-being which drives them to a better performance to the way communication between persons and departments occurs and the way flow of ideas is achieved inside the company. Another important thing about culture is that the right one is the one which has embedded factors like an out-of-the-box perception of things, maybe a flat hierarchy in order to help the flow of ideas from and to everybody, and of course a mentality which is focused in transformation, agility, and innovation. Small businesses that can adopt such a company culture will be able to deal in a better and more efficient way their potential problems, especially during financial crisis periods of time or when they need to operate in saturated markets or red oceans as we will see in Chapter 4.

Author's Notes

In this chapter we discussed about the liquidity problems that small businesses face in terms of how to confront them. We stressed the four sources of their financing, with an emphasis on angel investors and capital ventures.

We discussed whether small businesses need to embrace a cost-cutting approach or to continue their investment during crisis and difficult financial periods of time.

We also briefly surveyed the world of turnaround or sustainable reorganization, and we pinpointed the main factors that can lead a turnaround procedure to fail or to succeed.

Finally we had a brief discussion about innovation in SMEs. We underlined its importance, especially during difficult periods, and we stressed how important it is to have it embedded in the company's culture.

The main points to which we need to be focused on are the following:

- SMEs' financing sources (angel investors, capital venture, banking financing, owners' financing), their common characteristics and their differences
- Turnaround management
- Innovation and company culture

Suggested questions:

1. Which are the main financing sources that SMEs can use? What are their main characteristics, differences, and similarities?
2. Should SMEs follow a cost-cutting approach during turbulent times or not, and why?
3. What is turnaround management? Why is it so important for SMEs? Which are the factors that can lead to its implementation to decline or to succeed?
4. Why is innovation so important for SMEs? Which are some of the more important forms of innovation and why are they important? Do we need to embed innovation in the company's culture or not and why?

CHAPTER 5

Small Business and Blue Ocean Strategy

What is blue ocean strategy—its components and main characteristics. Value innovation. The strategy canvas. The four actions framework. Blue ocean strategy implementation in small business during financial crisis or in saturated markets.

5.1 The Concept of Blue Ocean Strategy

Blue ocean strategy is an approach that was first introduced by the INSEAD professors Kim and Mauborgne in 2005. It was, and still is, a very innovative approach in business, an approach which can help businesses when they are operating in saturated markets or during vast financial crisis.

According to Kim and Mauborgne (2005), if we suppose that all markets consist of the market universe, then this universe can be said to consist of two types of "oceans," the red oceans and the blue oceans. The red oceans comprise of all the known industries that exist today, while the blue oceans comprise of all the industries that do not exist today.

While red oceans are increasingly characterized by fierce competition and markets that usually are saturated, the blue oceans can be characterized as industries that are untouched and uncontested (Kim and Mauborgne 2005). See Table 5.1.

In the above table, we can see the composition of both blue and red oceans and their main characteristics.

The main idea of the blue ocean strategy concept is that companies in order to prosper in the future need to stop competing in saturated markets with fierce competition and to create their own new blue oceans by

Table 5.1 Blue ocean strategy, its composition, and its main characteristics (Kim and Mauborgne 2005)

Market Type	Composition	Characteristics
Red oceans	All the known industries that exist today.	Fierce competition and markets that usually are saturated. Industry boundaries are defined and accepted, and the competitive rules of the game are known.
Blue oceans	All the industries that do not exist today.	Industries that are untouched and uncontested. Demand is created rather than fought over. There is ample opportunity for growth that is both profitable and rapid.

creating new industries which are uncontested and where competition is made irrelevant (Kim and Mauborgne 2005).

In Table 5.2, we can see both oceans, red and blue, in terms of their characteristics in a more detailed form and in juxtaposition (Blueoceanstrategy.com n.d.).

Table 5.2 Blue oceans against red oceans (Blueoceanstrategy. com n.d.)

Red Oceans	Blue Oceans
Compete in existing marketplace	Create uncontested market space
Beat the competition	Make the competition irrelevant
Exploit existing demand	Create and capture new demand
Make the value-cost trade-off	Break the value-cost trade-off
Align the whole system of a firm's activities with its strategic choice of differentiation or low cost	Align the whole system of a firm's activities in pursuit of differentiation and low cost

In order for companies to implement the blue ocean strategy, they can use a series of tools which can help the company in question to discover its new market segment where competition is irrelevant and makes its business flourish.

These tools are the following (Blueoceanstrategy.com n.d.):
* Value innovation
* Strategy canvas
* Four actions framework
* Six paths framework

- Pioneer migrator settler map
- Three tiers of noncustomers
- Sequence of creating a blue ocean
- Buyer utility map

Although each of these tools is very important and can help business in many ways, the most important and most common are value innovation, the strategy canvas, and the four actions framework, which we will see in the following paragraphs.

Value innovation. The concept of value innovation is extremely important for all businesses and of course for SMEs. The creation of value for customers and in the long run for the company via the use of innovation is in a few lines what this concept involves. By pursuing simultaneously both differentiation and low cost, companies can evolve their market-creating strategy, or in other words, their blue ocean proposition (Blueoceanstrategy.com n.d.).

The aim of this concept is to align utility, price, and costs as value for customers comes from the offering's utility minus its price, while the company's "portion" of value comes from the offering's price minus its cost (Blueoceanstrategy.com n.d.).

The value innovation concept can be depicted in Figure 5.1:

- The cost savings can be made by completely eliminating and reducing the factors an industry competes on.
- Buyer value is increased by creating products or services that the existent industry has never offered before.

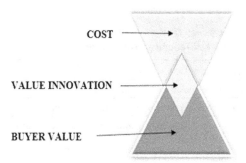

Figure 5.1 Value innovation

The strategy canvas. This can be seen as a central diagnostic tool and an action framework which vividly depicts both the current strategic positioning of the company and its future prospects (Blueoceanstrategy.com n.d.). Figure 5.2 gives a depiction of how this tool operates.

It has two axes, the horizontal one gives the elements that the specific industry competes on, while the vertical axis depicts the offering level that buyers receive across all these key competing elements (Blueoceanstrategy. com n.d.).

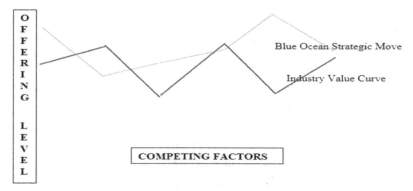

Figure 5.2 The strategy canvas

By using the strategy canvas, each organization can see in just one figure all the elements upon which the industry in question competes on and invests in, what customers receive as a final product, and what are the strategic moves/profile of the major competitors in the industry (Table 5.3).

Table 5.3 The purposes that strategy canvas serves as part of the blue ocean strategy (Blueoceanstrategy.com n.d.)

Strategy Canvas Main Purposes
Captures the current state of play in the industry in question.
Depicts in an indirect way the profiles of all the industry major players.
Re-orienting the user from competitors to alternatives and from customers to noncustomers.
Allows the company in question to visualize the blue ocean strategic move away from the existing red ocean.

The four actions framework. This tool, along with the others, was also developed and introduced by Kim and Mauborgne (2005). It is used in a way that it can reconstruct buyer value factors that will help the company in question to develop a new value curve or its new strategic profile (Blueoceanstrategy.com n.d.).

In order to use the framework toward the break of the trade-off between differentiation and low cost, something which inevitably will end up with the creation of a new value curve, this tool/method poses four key questions (Table 5.4) which can be proved quite challenging (Blueoceanstrategy.com n.d.).

Table 5.4 Four actions framework key questions (Blueoceanstrategy. com n.d.)

Raise	Which factors should be raised above the industry standards?
Eliminate	Which factors that the industry has long competed on should be eliminated?
Create	Which factors should be created that the industry has never offered?
Reduce	Which factors should be reduced well below the industry standards?

All the above-mentioned questions will lead to the creation of new value for the company, which will accordingly lead to the creation of its blue ocean by making competition irrelevant.

5.2 Blue Ocean Strategy Implementation in Small Business during Vast Financial Crisis or in Saturated Markets

SMEs, as mentioned earlier, are the backbone of each society. Their survival and growth are of the utmost importance for every society and economy. In order to be able to survive during crisis periods, SMEs need to be able to adapt to the new circumstances and to be ready to implement strategic movements that can bring them on a safe path. This is why blue ocean strategy can be a very powerful weapon in the hands of SME owners. Being able to implement a blue ocean strategy is not something which demands a huge investment as money can be derived via the decrease of the costs that are correlated with services that were offered while the company was competing in the red ocean. In other words, the whole concept can be seen as a form of restructuring business via innovation and new market creation.

In the value innovation strategic tool we saw that value can be achieved via innovation. As Carsten (2008) stresses, innovation should be seen as, and surely is, the foundation of conducting business and producing new goods and services. It is imperative for all companies to innovate at least at one point during their life cycle in order to remain competitive (Carsten 2008). Especially nowadays due to the globalization of markets as the competition became stiff, companies need to innovate more than ever in order to access domestic markets by overcoming the barriers that incumbents impose (Carsten 2008).

As the importance of innovation and thus value innovation and accordingly blue ocean strategy was highlighted in the previous paragraph by Carsten (2008), we need to understand that SMEs often search for a specific market niche which can be attained by product differentiation, something which probably will give them the competitive advantage they need in order to survive in today's competitive markets and thrive (Carsten 2008).

So, till now, SME managers in order to attain such differentiation used methods like cost cutting or product differentiation, or even services and processes differentiation in order to be able to find that niche they were looking for (Carsten 2008). Under this prism, we need to say that the blue ocean approach seems extremely suitable for SMEs of all kinds. It can help them find the niche they are looking for, while they don't need to invest money, especially during turbulent times, in creating new processes and services. On the other hand, cost reduction will be inevitable as the company will no longer be in need of its previous budgets which had to do with expenses that were originated in the needs of the market that consisted of the red ocean where the company was competing and which, after the implementation of the blue ocean, will no longer exist, making the competition irrelevant.

Lai et al. (2011) also underline in their paper that SMEs in order to be able to find their niche according to their unique advantages toward the development of high-margin products through product customization strategies can use the blue ocean strategy.

Papazov and Mihaylova (2016) in a research that they conducted in the knitwear industry in Bulgaria came to the result that blue ocean strategy can successfully be used by SMEs.

Another interesting perspective of how blue ocean strategy can be utilized in SMEs around the globe in order to help them avoid pitfalls, especially when times are difficult and financial problems arise, can be found in the research that was conducted by Negoescu in 2011.

Negoescu (2011) underlines that during the years between 2008 and 2011, Romanian SMEs were facing many financial problems, which led to more than 60,000 bankruptcies and 200,000 firm suspensions, facts that inevitably led to an increase of unemployment from 568,000 (December 31, 2008) to 711,000 (June 30, 2011). The author argues that blue ocean strategy via the use of tools such as the strategic sail and the EDDC matrix which were developed by Kim and Mauborgne (2005) can be very critical in helping SMEs avoid bankruptcy, or at least to reduce the risk they suffer by being exposed in such situations (Negoescu 2011).

As we saw in this chapter, implementing the blue ocean strategy approach can be crucial in terms of helping small businesses overcome their recession problems and drive their growth toward their sustainable development as we will see in Chapter 6.

Author's Notes

The blue ocean strategy should be very important for any contemporary business, especially for small business which struggles to survive during financially turbulent times.

This chapter is an introduction to the blue ocean strategy theory as it can be seen like a unique way that small businesses can use in order to survive and achieve their competitive advantage which accordingly will bring them closer to their sustainable development in the long run.

Main points:

- What is the blue ocean strategy? What are its main characteristics?
- The tools that blue ocean strategy is using.
- The role of innovation in blue ocean strategy.
- Blue ocean strategy implementation.

Suggested questions:

1. What is the blue ocean strategy? What are its main characteristics?
2. What are the differences and the similarities between blue and red oceans?
3. What is the role of innovation in creation of value innovation, and in the implementation of blue ocean strategy in general?
4. Which are the main tools that the blue ocean strategy uses?
5. How can the blue ocean strategy help small businesses find their niche that they are looking for to operate?
6. How can we implement the blue ocean strategy successfully?

CHAPTER 6

Small Business Sustainable Development

Company's sustainable development. Six emerging organizational culture development practices which lead to small business sustainable development. Innovation toward sustainable development. Innopreneurial spirit in small business. Sustainable development and corporate social responsibility in small business.

6.1 Paragons Involved in Small Business Sustainable Development

Tsai and Chou (2009) stress that sustainable development, especially in the last years, has become a very important factor for companies around the globe, as it can bring growth and prosperity. They stressed that especially for small business and entrepreneurial orientations (SMEs) in order to help them create sustainable competitive advantage and thus their sustainable development, there are four management systems, namely ISO 9001, ISO 14001, OHSAS 18001, and SA 8000 (Tsai and Chou 2009).

An important factor which can play a vital role in the company's sustainable development, as we saw in Chapter 5, is company culture.

Nuttasom Ketprapakorn and Sooksan Kantabutra (2019), in their study analysis, found that small companies can achieve sustainable development by adapting specific traits of behavior in terms of the company's culture. These traits/practices are depicted in Table 6.1.

Table 6.1 Six emerging organizational culture development practices which lead to small business sustainable development (Ketprapakorn and Kantabutra 2019)

Organizational Cultural Practices for SMEs Toward Sustainable Development
Virtues, social and environmental responsibility, and innovation are the company's core values.
The company's leaders need to act as role models according to the abovementioned values.
Companies need to grow their own managers in order to be able to continue their corporate culture.
Designing the communication channels of the company in a way that they can emphasize the core values among employees.
While recruiting new employees, the abovementioned company core values should be the main criteria for the decision.
Avoiding employee layoff in order to be able to preserve the valuable corporate core values, even when things are not good (i.e., during years of financial crisis).

In their pilot study on regionally based SMEs in Poland, Malik and Jasińka-Biliczak (2018) tried to focus on processes that can be used as instruments by SMEs in order to be able to implement the models needed to help them achieve their sustainable development. They argue that the state of enterprises can be highly affected by their embedded ability to classify processes and the occurrences inside these processes (Malik and Jasińka-Biliczak 2018).

Under this prism, they also underline that innovation is a crucial factor which facilitates the SMEs' sustainable development, while this has to do with how entrepreneurs realize the innovation process per se (Malik and Jasińka-Biliczak 2018). So, they argue, that as a result of their research, there is a huge need among SME owners to understand that awareness needs to be raised in terms of the fact that innovation needs to be treated as a process in itself which often can be seen as the sum of other supporting processes that take place inside an enterprise and that toward the sustainable development direction, there is a huge need for knowledge to be transferred from experts outside SMEs to SMEs (Malik and Jasińka-Biliczak 2018).

In terms of how innovation can assist sustainable development, especially and specifically in SMEs, Guo-Ciang (2017) stresses there are several categories of sustainability-oriented innovations (SOIs). Such categories, although difficult to be implemented by SMEs due to the fact that they often lack in resources, play an important part in amplifying sustainability in economic, environmental, and social sectors (Guo-Ciang 2017).

The importance of sustainable development in SMEs is also underlined by Salimzadeh and Courvisanos (2015). In their paper "A Conceptual Framework for Assessing Sustainable Development in Regional SMEs," the authors argue that as SMEs are a significant regional development agent, if they will be able to adopt sustainability and regional economic strategies at the same time, they will be able to provide more via their social responsibility actions to the local community as it will benefit from their sustainable development, innovation, and economic development as a result of the former in their region (Salimzadeh and Courvisanos 2015).

Another research conducted in Benin (Tokognon and Shao 2018) is in the same wavelength as it indicates that innovation, which is a very important aspect for large enterprises as well, can be said that it is the cornerstone of SMEs' sustainable development, thus growth. Although sustainable development can be achieved for both small and large businesses via innovation, it is easier and most often to be seen in large corporations. This is underlined in a research which was conducted in Lithuanian SMEs by Kęstutis and Greblikaitė (2007), who stress that SMEs are less innovative than large corporations. This fact per se is indicative of many pathogeneses that small businesses can carry like the way small business owners perceive the role of innovation in their business, or the culture which small businesses usually adapt, which often is away from any innovative framework.

Another important aspect to take into consideration is that sustainable development needs to be achieved from an environmental perspective. Entrepreneurship needs to be innopreneurship[1] in a greater degree and small businesses need to approach environmentally sensitive fields via their corporate social responsibility more often, by using technologies that reduce the impact of ecological footprint, or that are capable of generating natural resources.

It is imperative here to say that it is very important that sustainable development should not only pass via corporate social responsibility by having a vast positive impact to the society as SMEs are vivid parts

---

[1]Innopreneurs: Innopreneurship is the teaching and the practice of entrepreneurial action which aims in the transformation of new findings in terms of scientific, technical, and organizational findings into marketable products and services, and also their successful establishment as novelties into the market where the company operates. The personal attitude that brings such actions into reality can be referred to as innopreneurial spirit, while the people who demonstrate such spirit are usually called innopreneurs (Joernlengsfeld.com n.d.).

of such societies, but it also has to be achieved via a sensitive approach to environment, especially nowadays that we face global phenomena which are indicative of the mistreatment of the environment on a global scale.

Achieving their sustainable development and surviving during turbulent periods of time, although of utmost importance for the SMEs, is not a panacea. It cannot lead to a brighter future if it will result in environmental problems against the company's corporate social responsibility. Companies in general need to operate in a way that they understand the needs of their surrounding societal frame and the needs of people and the planet as a whole.

The importance of the environmental impact of all the actions taken from SMEs toward sustainable development is highlighted also in the paper by Medakovic and Vaskovic (2015), which has its main focus on production, distribution, and consumption of energy as part of the concept of sustainability.

These factors are very important for the development of each country and as the concept of sustainable development has grown in the last years, companies started to target new forms of energy like the renewable ones in order to meet their energy needs (Medakovic and Vaskovic 2015). As the global need for a total rebirth of our planet increases and environmental concerns are in the frontline of all media, the whole world needs to understand that it is very important that while SMEs are struggling toward their sustainable development, that should be done only by following sustainable trends in production, consumption, social relations, and habits of people and that they need to establish their growth only by having as cornerstone of their development such mentality and approach to things (Medakovic and Vaskovic 2015).

Another tool that can be used extremely effectively in SMEs in order to help them toward the achievement of their sustainable development is the so-called performance management (PM) systems.[2]

PMs have become a crucial part of SMEs toward their sustainable development, especially during crucial economic transition periods (Bianchi et al. 2014). The authors stress that an important paragon in the whole

---

[2]Performance management systems: Performance management is the very process that provides the team with accountability, feedback, and documentation for performance outcomes. It is a process/system that is able to help employees to channel their talents toward the given organizational goals (Gallant 2012).

concept of sustainable development achievement in SMEs is the improvement of decision-maker strategic learning processes, during which the traditional PM frameworks need to be combined with the so-called system dynamics (SD) modeling[3] (Bianchi et al. 2014).

Krishnan and Ganesh (2014) stress how important it is for all companies and especially for SMEs to achieve their sustainable development, especially in a way that via their corporate social responsibility they will be able to help toward societal sustainability as well. Implementing a sustainability development model thus can be a very challenging situation for all SMEs even when what they formally claim indicates a strict adoption of the main principles of sustainable development itself (Markey 2010, cited in Krishnan and Ganesh 2014). Identifying sustainable development principles as an important community vision is something that needs a lot of attention, while the main problem is that SMEs which are into it have difficulties in translating their goals into real-life strategy via implementation (Markey 2010, cited in Krishnan and Ganesh 2014).

Sustainable development is a very important goal that SMEs are seeking throughout their lifetime. As described previously, they can reach it via certain ways which of course are not very easy to follow. In their research, Dee and Jones (2016) underline that the provision of organizational development[4] and learning OD/L programs that are based on both the collaboration and learning resulted in positive ways for SME owners, while in the long run, they had also positive effects in paragons like business confidence, clarity, and action which are crucial for SMEs' overall operation (Dee and Jones 2016). Dee and Jones (2016) also stress that such an approach also has social implications, which are derived from the fact that demonstrating support to SME business owners in a rather targeted way, in socially deprived areas, can result in increasing

---

[3]System Dynamics (SD): Is a computer-aided procedure toward policy analysis and design. It can be applied to dynamic problems which arise in complex social, managerial, economic, or even ecological systems, generally speaking, in all dynamic systems which are characterized by independence, mutual interaction, information feedback, and circular causality (systemdynamics.org n.d.).

[4]Organizational Development: This is a loosely defined field of practice and inquiry which represents the goal of improving organizations in order to make them more effective (Basadur and Licina 2012).

the potential for growth, while in parallel economic regeneration is also positively influenced.

In terms of how SMEs operate in their pursuit for sustainable development, something which has positive implications on societal level, a paragon which is very important is how they handle their product development.

Barkan, Gunnarsson, and Postel (2010) underline in their case study which used an SME in the manufacturing industry with customers and office locations globally as their case, stating that product development in SMEs is a paragon that is extremely crucial in terms of how to leverage it toward societal sustainability. By using a participatory action research approach in their abovementioned research, they concluded that if an SME needs to move toward sustainability, it has to adopt a repetition of the process it follows with its used Method for Sustainable Product Development (MSPD)[5] and also to use additional tools which can be used as a supplement to that MSPD method (Barkan, Gunnarsson, and Postel 2010).

Another very crucial point that we need to underline is that the human factor is very important in terms of how SMEs are going to operate. In the same vein, sustainability is something that is influenced a lot from a factor called leadership.

Under this prism, Szczepańska-Woszczyna and Kurowska-Pysz (2016) stress in their quantitative research analysis—which examined a sample of 138 managers and SMEs' representatives located in Poland in 2015— that leadership is a major aspect in terms of influencing sustainability in an SME. The researchers argue that there is a statistically significant relationship between taking action in an SME and the awareness that the

---

[5]Sustainable Product Development: When we deal with sustainable product development, it means that we have to consider factors like the environment, production, regulatory and economic paragons that intervene with the production, use, and disposal of products. When we refer to sustainable new product development, we need to underline that it is an integral part of the whole procedure of innovation and of course the new product development lifecycle, which begins with the inclusion of sustainability principles and goals embedded in a company's strategic business objectives as a whole (Sopheon.com n.d.).

company's managers have regarding the very concept of sustainable development (Szczepańska-Woszczyna and Kurowska-Pysz 2016).

Another important factor that can prove extremely influential for SMEs' sustainable development process is the influence of managers on employees and additionally, the stimulation of their behavior which includes development, decent treatment of employees, the way employees communicate with their managers toward common goals, and finally the system of rewards and promotions as part of the company's overall management control systems (MCS)[6] that are adapted by the company (Szczepańska-Woszczyna and Kurowska-Pysz 2016).

As can be seen from the above, sustainable development for a small business, and for any business, should be something that as a process and as an idea need to be embedded deeply in the company's culture and also needs to be communicated effectively to both employees and stakeholders. As the goal can be achieved, via the use of the right MCS, it is imperative that such systems need to operate in the right way, which is the employees' overall positive experience as part of the company via the right company culture.

As managers are interacting with their employees in terms of developing them toward the common goal which is the company's sustainable development, thus growth and as they are interacting toward the same direction with external stakeholders, their presence is very important toward the sustainable development of their small business (Szczepańska-Woszczyna and Kurowska-Pysz 2016).

Another critical point regarding SMEs' sustainable development is how it can be achieved while SMEs are in a difficult situation (i.e., financial problem, etc.) and having problems using their already scarce resources. As SMEs are in trouble getting financing in, generally speaking,

---

[6]Management Control Systems: Management Control Systems are both the formal and informal structures that a company puts in place as part of its whole operational procedure, which are used to compare the strategy the organization has implemented to the actual outcomes as a result of the employees' efforts. In other words, such systems are used to measure how well the functions of the business as a whole perform and meet the given objectives which are aligned with the company's strategy. After the management reviews this comparison, it is able to take the necessary decisions in order to achieve the best possible outcome (Myaccountingcourse.com n.d.a).

especially difficult financial situations, like during crisis years, it is difficult for them to be able to gather the resources needed in order to develop the appropriate innovations that will enhance their sustainable development (Halme and Korpela 2014). So, the question is whether SMEs can achieve the sustainable development that they seek via the appropriate innovation by only using the scarce resources that they have in hand (Halme and Korpela 2014).

Continuing their research, Halme and Korpela (2014) underline that SMEs are capable of achieving their sustainable development goals via creative innovations by using their scarce resources through a very different resource combination. Such a combination comprises equity, research, and development cooperation, the use of networks, their acquired industry knowledge, and their established reputation (Halme and Korpela 2014).

So, reaching the company's sustainable development goals via creative innovation, even for SMEs which suffer from their scarce resources problem, which usually has to do mainly with their financing, can be possible if the right combination of their scarce resources can be used in order to fill the resources gap. As the saying goes, "where there is a problem, there is also a solution." So it is important to understand that SMEs, regardless of their possible difficult situation in terms of financing, can leverage their power via different approaches in order to be able to sustain and grow, even during the most difficult situations, something which is a very hopeful and positive message globally.

Another important point of sustainable development in all companies, and of course in SMEs which is in huge correlation with the company's corporate social responsibility approach is that the key target of sustainable development should be the company's target for high environmental performance in combination with economic and social effectiveness (Laurinkevičiūtė and Stasiškienė 2011). Such sustainable development which has its focus on the company's positive environmental and social profile is mainly based on preventive management principles. How such a management approach is implemented to SMEs can be a vital component of enhancing SMEs' competitiveness, as it is a very important paragon involved in the whole process of SMEs' achievement of sustainable development (Laurinkevičiūtė and Stasiškienė 2011).

Following a sensitive environment profile, small businesses will acquire a grip on the society in which they are operating. This, in the long run, will help them establish a customer-friendly face and will even increase their brand visibility, things which will help the company in the long run to achieve its sustainable development targets and will inevitably help it to overcome the crisis that it might face. It is like doing something good and that good will return to you somehow, although in business this "somehow" is translated into customer retention, brand awareness, and revenue.

But what is really "preventive management" or as it is also known "preventive maintenance"? Preventive management, or preventive maintenance, is maintenance that is regularly performed on an equipment in order to help lessen the possibilities of its failure (fixsoftware.com n.d.).

According to the same source, there are two types of preventive maintenance, the time-based one and the usage-based one. The first one refers to scheduled timely maintenance as in regular time laps, while the second one refers to the maintenance intervention that happens after a certain usage of the machinery.

Preventive maintenance is a powerful tool in the hands of SME managers who are trying to achieve the company's strategic goals which involve, among other things, the company's sustainable development. Under this prism, preventive maintenance can be extremely helpful for the company which is trying to meet its contemporary and future needs. In Table 6.2, we can see the main types of preventive maintenance.

Table 6.2 Types of preventive maintenance (fixsoftware.com n.d.)

Types of Preventive Maintenance/Management
Time-based preventive maintenance
Usage-based preventive maintenance

Laurinkevičiūtė and Stasiškienė (2011) try to unveil the decision process that SMEs are following toward their sustainable development targets. They argue that SMEs in order to be able to make decision on a sustainable basis should not only improve the company's overall environmental performance, but also be effective in both their economic and social agenda, as they need to use an integrated sustainable management system (SMS)[7] (Laurinkevičiūtė and Stasiškienė 2011). Such SMS needs to be based on financial analysis and to be oriented toward the company's strategic sustainability goals, without requiring the use of significant financial and human resources (Laurinkevičiūtė and Stasiškienė 2011).

Such systems in order to be implemented and integrated properly need to be comprised of five essential phases, each of which is crucial in evaluating the organizational achievements in a period which usually is a year (12 months). These five critical phases are depicted in Table 6.3:

Table 6.3 The five phases of SMS (Eticambiente.com n.d.)

The Five Phases of a Sustainability Management System
Reviewing: a starting point for future comparisons
Defining: short-, medium-, and long-term objectives
Aligning: vision, programs, and management systems
Ensuring: staff and partners' contributions and actions
Monitoring: results and impact of outcome reporting

Limited environmental and social resources including financial ones is a major problem for SMEs all around the globe. It is possible for them to achieve sustainable development even under such a situation. Hatak, Floh, and Zauner (2015) stress that even under such circumstances of lack of resources, SMEs should be able to drive their sustainable development through new products or services. The problem in such circumstances is, as they state, that it is considerably uncertain how SMEs will be able to discover, develop, and realize sustainability-related opportunities in their organizations in order to be able to achieve their sustainable development targets (Hatak, Floh, and Zauner 2015).

---

[7]Sustainability Management System (SMS): "An integrated SMS is a management system that authentically unifies as a whole an organization in its entirety, and integrates its systems and processes into one complete, cohesive framework by adopting a holistic approach and a common set of documentation, policies, procedures, and processes that enable all internal and external staff and management to work as a single unit, all while helping deliver organization's objectives effectively and efficiently" (Eticambiente.com n.d.).

As we saw all over the sustainable development of SMEs, one of the main pillars upon which SMEs' sustainable development is based, is the environment. Henriques and Catarino (2015) stress that eco-efficiency is critical for small business as its main aim is to improve the economic and ecological efficiency of the company in question, to attain higher value with less inputs, which usually are materials and energy, and in general the main target for the company is to achieve more output with less possible waste (Henriques and Catarino 2015).

They name this company value through sustainable development, "sustainable value concept" and it represents higher company value, which can be defined as the relationship between the satisfaction of needs and the resources used to achieve this satisfaction and finally, as a result, the increase in the company's overall competitiveness (Henriques and Catarino 2015). The authors argue that if a small business company will be able to achieve this concept, the results will integrate the three aspects of sustainable development—economic, environmental, and social development (Henriques and Catarino 2015). In figure 6.1, we can see a depiction of the components of sustainable development as they are presented by Henriques and Catarino (2015).

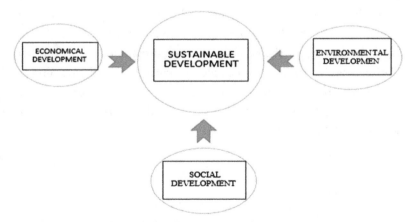

Figure 6.1 The three components of sustainable development (Henriques and Catarino 2015)

Quaye and Mensah (2019) found that product design and packaging innovations in combination with promotion innovations, retail innovations, and pricing innovations can provide specific SMEs that deal with water, beverage, detergent, and metal fabrication, a sustainable market advantage. They add that product designs and product packages combined with retail outlets are the most important components that provide to the abovementioned SMEs the competitive advantage they are seeking (Quaye and Mensah 2019).

Such components are extremely important for all SMEs as they are capable of giving to the companies in question the power to overcome all obstacles that bad financing or saturated markets might impose on them, especially during crisis periods. They can also provide them with the ability to reach their targeted sustainable development even with only the use of their scarce resources, something which is extremely important.

Quaye and Mensah (2019) also underline that the combination of marketing resources and marketing capabilities with innovative marketing activities can show small businesses the way to increase their competitive advantage in order to achieve sustainable development.

In their research conducted via a survey of 241 SMEs which were operating in the manufacturing industry in Philippines, Roxas and Chadee (2016) indicate that the role of knowledge management (KM)[8] in helping small businesses to be able to engage in environmentally sustainable business is huge. The authors stress that SMEs, which have to utilize their constrained resources, mostly rely on their relational capital in order to be able to innovate toward environmental ways of operating (Roxas and Chadee 2016). They conclude that using their KM capabilities is crucial in order to reach their target (Roxas and Chadee 2016).

---

[8]Knowledge Management: It can be defined as the systematic management of an organization's knowledge assets in order to create value and to meet the company's strategic and tactical requirements as they were posed by the company's management. Its main components are the following:

Initiatives, processes, strategies, systems that sustain and enhance the company's storage, assessment, sharing, refinement, and knowledge creation (knowledge-management-tools.net 2018).

Author's Notes

Sustainable development is something which can be seen as the ultimate goal for every company and especially for SMEs. It is something that guarantees its present and future adequate function. Its importance is huge, especially during financial crisis years and this is why all companies struggle to achieve it one way or another.

In this chapter we discussed about sustainable development, what it is, its main components, and how it can be achieved by small business.

Main points:

The main points of this chapter are the following:

- Four management systems toward sustainable development
- Company culture
- Six emerging organizational culture development practices toward sustainable development
- Innovation/innopreneurship
- Environmental impact of sustainable development
- Organizational development and organizational development learning
- Methods of sustainable product development
- Leadership
- Preventive management and high environmental performance toward sustainable development
- The three components of sustainable development.

Suggested questions:

1. What do we mean by the term sustainable development? Why is it so important for small businesses during financial crisis periods?
2. Which are the four management systems that small businesses can use toward their sustainable development?
3. Which are the six emerging organizational culture development practices which can lead small businesses to their sustainable development?
4. What do we call "performance management systems"?

5. What is the method for sustainable product development (MSPD)? Why it is so important for small business sustainable development?

6. What is the role of leadership in small business sustainable development?

7. What are the principles of preventive management and why are they so important for small businesses during crisis periods?

8. Which are the five phases of sustainability management systems?

9. Which are the three components of sustainable development?

Epilogue

SMEs are the backbone of all societies worldwide. Their survival, especially during financially difficult years, is of utmost importance, not only for them but also for the societies in which they operate.

In this book, we presented a thorough view of what SMEs are, how they need to operate during difficult periods, and what they need to do in order to be able to sustain and survive during such periods.

A very important factor which is the main pillar upon which small businesses should operate in order to survive is to be based on an entrepreneurial orientation. Upon this base, they need to also develop their strategy formulation.

Another important paragon that can be crucial for small businesses during crisis years is the way SME owners perceive things—in other words, the small business owners' mentality. Their way of thinking is crucial because at the end of the day they will be the ones who will take the decisions regarding their company's strategy, culture, and operations in general.

As SMEs are facing so many risks during crisis periods, they need to develop the right risk management mechanisms. Research on several levels showed that although SME owners understand the risks that they need to deal with, in reality they only try to implement informal risk management mechanisms which to a certain extent tend to be based on their intuition and experience. This way of approaching things has to do a lot with their mentality, knowledge, and of course with the company's financial situation, which might be preventive in terms of cutting costs during crisis years. The important thing is that they need to rethink the way they perceive their cost-cutting approach, if that is the case, because risk management mechanisms can be said to be the company's firewall against outside threats.

Credit risk is another paragon which can have a negative impact on SMEs' financing, especially during turbulent times. When they turn to the banking financing, they need to have a good credit score in order to get the financing they need. In that pursuit of financing, it is important to choose the right bank that fits their needs and to be able to present a good credit score, something which has to do with their current liquidity, their previous and already running loans, and their precarious assets.

In order to be able to survive, SME owners sometimes tend to be tempted in terms of being tax compliant or not. Tax compliance is a very important issue as it does have a vast impact not only in SMEs' operations but also in the society as a whole, as it influences negatively the tax collection which can create deficiencies in the states operations and accordingly in the society in terms of its development and additional taxes that might be imposed by the state in order to cover the created tax–income gap. On the other hand, SMEs that are not tax compliant might face high fines that will be imposed on them because of their behavior. Such fines, especially when liquidity is a problem, might be the company's tombstone and lead to bankruptcy.

Whatever small businesses might do in terms of how to operate during crisis years, the alpha and the omega of their whole existence is their company culture. The advent of A.I. leaves no choice for small businesses that usually cannot support technological investments of any kind in order to become competitive against large companies that are in better financial position. SMEs need to create a great company culture in order to make their employees feel good in what they are doing and in order not only to retain them but also to attract the best ones. In addition, if employees feel great, they will inevitably increase their productivity and will become a great asset for the company in question, something which will help it to be competitive in the long run. The importance of the right company culture is huge and is something which not only needs to begin from the top of the hierarchy, which usually is the owner of the small business, but also needs to be communicated throughout the company both vertically and horizontally in the best possible way in order to be implemented effectively.

In the same wavelength, small businesses also need to have a customer-centric approach embedded in their company culture in order to retain their customers and to be able to be competitive enough toward their survival during crisis periods. Retained customers are a source of revenue when times are difficult, not to mention that they are the very reason why the company operates in the first place. We need not forget that we are living in the era of social media and Internet and that a satisfied customer might have even hundreds of thousands of followers, so word of mouth might work in an exponentially way.

As we saw earlier, SMEs have the banking sector as their main source of financing. Although that seems obvious, it is not always the case, especially during difficult financial times. The example of the recent big financial crisis in Greece when banks stopped financing small businesses or, at best, reduced a lot of their financing while capital controls were implemented in order to control the money flow all over the country is a quite characteristic one. There are other sources of financing which can help SMEs when needed and need to be considered by them equally if they want to survive during difficult periods.

As they want to survive and turn around their business, SMEs need to exercise practices like the turn-around management and the blue ocean strategy one. Especially the blue ocean strategy is a strategic approach which can be vital for small businesses as it can help them when markets are saturated or businesses are not moving forward due to financial issues. Examples like the "Cirque du Soleil" are characteristic of how blue ocean strategy can help small businesses to make the competition irrelevant, cut unnecessary costs, and re-organize their business; thus, small businesses not only survive during turbulent periods but also even thrive by re-inventing its business and create value for its customers.

In order for small businesses to be able to change their approach in terms of how to operate or how they are facing their business problems and inadequacies, they need to embed into their culture an innovation mentality. Innovation is the cornerstone of change and since change is something that small businesses need to consider during periods of crisis, it is imperative for them to have an innovative spirit.

The main goal of all businesses is the profit of course, but in order for this profit to be able to help them grow in the long run, in reality their main goal is their sustainable development. So, sustainable development can be seen as the way small businesses, try to face positively their current crisis situation, not only financially but also operationally. This will result into their business development on the long run. In other words, "sustainable development" is the development via sustainability achievement.

It is imperative that small businesses facing turbulent periods adapt all the above-mentioned measures which will be able to strengthen their operations, their mentality, and their strategic decisions and lead them toward their sustainable development, which is their number one target. Although financing may be their biggest problem, especially during difficult periods, they need to be able to see the big picture, which is a better way of functioning as organizations and as a team, and even a restructuring of their business in order to make even their financing problem irrelevant.

References

Aksoy, H. 2017. "How Do Innovation Culture, Marketing Innovation and Product Innovation Affect the Market Performance of Small and Medium-Sized Enterprises (SMEs)?" *Technology in Society* 51, pp. 133-41.

Aloulou, W. and A. Fayolle. 2005. "A Conceptual Approach of Entrepreneurial Orientation within Small Business Context." *Journal of Enterprising Culture*, 13, no. 1, pp. 21-45.

Anagnostopoulos, n.d. "Springer Reference—LISREL," www.researchgate.net/publication/323683239_LISREL, (accessed 8 September 2019).

Andersén, J., Institutionen för handel och företagande, Högskolan i Skövde, and Forskningsspecialiseringen Framtidens Företagande. 2017. "What about the Employees in Entrepreneurial Firms? A Multi-Level Analysis of the Relationship between Entrepreneurial Orientation, Role Ambiguity, and Social Support." *International Small Business Journal: Researching Entrepreneurship* 35, no. 8, pp. 969-90.

Arend, R.J. 2014. "Social and Environmental Performance at SMEs: Considering Motivations, Capabilities, and Instrumentalism." *Journal of Business Ethics* 125, no. 4, pp. 541-61.

Ausloos, M., R. Cerqueti, F. Bartolacci, and N.G. Castellano. 2018. "SME Investment Best Strategies. Outliers for Assessing how to Optimize Performance." *Physica A: Statistical Mechanics and its Applications*, 509, pp. 754-65.

Bai, Y., J. Yuan, and J. Pan. 2017. "Why SMEs in Emerging Economies are Reluctant to Provide Employee Training: Evidence from China." *International Small Business Journal: Researching Entrepreneurship* 35, no. 6, pp. 751-66.

Baker, W.E. and J.M. Sinkula. 2009. "The Complementary Effects of Market Orientation and Entrepreneurial Orientation on Profitability in Small Businesses." *Journal of Small Business Management* 47, no. 4, pp. 443-64.

Barkan, A., D. Gunnarsson, and O. Postel. 2010. *Strategic Sustainable Product Development: A Case of an SME in the Sealing Industry*, Blekinge Tekniska Högskola, Sektionen för ingenjörsvetenskap.

Basadur, M. and G. Licina. 2012. "Organizational Development," www.sciencedirect.com/topics/neuroscience/organizational-development, (accessed 11 September 2019).

Battisti, M. and D. Deakins. 2018. "Microfoundations of Small Business Tax Behaviour: A Capability Perspective." *British Journal of Management* 29, no. 3, pp. 497-513.

Belas, J., L. Smrcka, B. Gavurova, and J. Dvorsky. 2018. "The Impact of Social and Economic Factors in the Credit Risk Management of SME." *Technological and Economic Development of Economy* 24, no. 3, pp. 1215-30.

Berger, A.N., G.M. Cerqueiro, and M. Penas. 2015. "Market Size Structure and Small Business Lending: Are Crisis Times Different from Normal Times?" *Review of Finance* 19, no. 5, pp. 1965-95.

Berk, A. 2017. "Small Business Social Responsibility: More than Size." *The Journal of Corporate Citizenship* 67, pp. 12-38.

Beyer, C. 2015. "Risk Management for Human Capital," http://insurancethoughtleadership.com/risk-management-for-human-capital/, (accessed 6 September 2019).

Bhasin, H. 2019. "What is Turnaround Management?" www.marketing91.com/what-is-turnaround-management/, (accessed 28 September 2019).

Bianchi, C., F. Cosenz, and M. Marinkovi. 2014. "Designing Dynamic Performance Management Systems to Foster SME Competitiveness According to a Sustainable Development Perspective: Empirical Evidences from a Case-Study." *International Journal of Business Performance Management* 16, no. 1, p. 84.

Blackburn, R.A., M. Hart, and T. Wainwright. 2013. "Small Business Performance: Business, Strategy and Owner-Manager Characteristics." *Journal of Small Business and Enterprise Development* 20, no. 1, pp. 8-27.

Blueoceanstrategy.com, n.d. "What is Blue Ocean Strategy?" www .blueoceanstrategy.com/what-is-blue-ocean-strategy/, (accessed 4 September 2019).

Bornman, M. and L. Stack. 2015. "Rewarding Tax Compliance: Taxpayers' Attitudes and Beliefs." *Journal of Economic and Financial Sciences* 8, no. 3, pp. 791-807.

Brunninge, O., M. Nordqvist, and J. Wiklund. 2007. "Corporate Governance and Strategic Change in SMEs: The Effects of Ownership, Board Composition and Top Management Teams." *Small Business Economics* 29, no. 3, pp. 295-308.

Brustbauer, J. 2016. "Enterprise Risk Management in SMEs: Towards a Structural Model." *International Small Business Journal* 34, no. 1, pp. 70-85.

Businessdictionary.com, n.d. "Innovation," www.businessdictionary.com/ definition/innovation.html, (accessed 28 September 2019).

Bussmann, K.D. and A. Niemeczek. 2019. "Compliance through Company Culture and Values: An International Study Based on the Example of Corruption Prevention." *Journal of Business Ethics* 157, no. 3, pp. 797-811.

Bussmann, K.D., A. Niemeczek, and M. Vockrodt. 2018. "Company Culture and Prevention of Corruption in Germany, China and Russia." *European Journal of Criminology* 15, no. 3, pp. 255-77.

Carbó-Valverde, S., F. Rodríguez-Fernández, and G.F. Udell. 2016. "Trade Credit, the Financial Crisis, and SME Access to Finance." *Journal of Money, Credit and Banking* 48, no. 1: pp. 113-43.

Carland, J.W., F. Hoy, W.R. Boulton, and J.A.C. Carland. 1984. "Differentiating Entrepreneurs from Small Business Owners: A Conceptualization." *The Academy of Management Review* 9, no. 2, pp. 354-9.

Carsten, S. 2008. *Blue Ocean Strategy for Small and Mid-Sized Companies in Germany: Development of a Consulting Approach.* 1. Aufl. Ed. DE: Diplomica Verlag GmbH.

Chesbrough, H.W., W. Vanhaverbeke, and J. West. 2006. *Open Innovation: Researching a New Paradigm.* New ed. Oxford: Oxford University Press.

Collett, N., N.R. Pandit, and J. Saarikko. 2014. "Success and Failure in Turnaround Attempts: An Analysis of SMEs within the

Finnish Restructuring of Enterprises Act." *Entrepreneurship & Regional Development* 26, nos. 1-2, pp. 123-41.

Corporate Finance Institute, n.d. "Diseconomies of Scale: Forces that Increase the Per-Unit Cost of Goods and Services," https://corporate-financeinstitute.com/resources/knowledge/economics/diseconomies-of-scale/, (accessed 27 June 2019).

Cowling, M., W. Liu, and N. Zhang. 2016. "Access to Bank Finance for UK SMEs in the Wake of the Recent Financial Crisis." *International Journal of Entrepreneurial Behavior & Research* 22, no. 6, pp. 903-32.

Daisuke T. 2015. "Bank Loan Availability and Trade Credit for Small Businesses during the Financial Crisis." *Quarterly Review of Economics and Finance* 55, pp. 40-52.

Decker, C. 2018. "Stakeholders' Impact on Turnaround Performance: The Case of German Savings Banks." *Journal of Small Business Management* 56, no. 4, pp. 534-54.

Dee, G. and K.F. Jones. 2016. "Using Organisational Development and Learning Methods to Develop Resilience for Sustainable Futures with SMEs and Micro Businesses: The Case of the Business Alliance." *Journal of Small Business and Enterprise Development* 23, no. 2, p. 474.

Deyoung, R., A. Gron, G. Torna, and A. Winton. 2015. "Risk Overhang and Loan Portfolio Decisions: Small Business Loan Supply before and during the Financial Crisis." *The Journal of Finance* 70, no. 6, pp. 2451-87.

Entrepreneur.com, n.d. "Trade Credit-Definition," www.entrepreneur.com/encyclopedia/trade-credit, (accessed 5 August 2019).

Eticambiente.com, n.d. "The 5 Components of Sustainability Management Systems," www.eticambiente.com/2011/01/14/top-5-components-of-a-sustainability-management-system/, (accessed 12 September 2019).

Ferreira, J.J., A. Fayolle, C. Fernandes, and M. Raposo. 2017. "Effects of Schumpeterian and Kirznerian Entrepreneurship on Economic Growth: Panel Data Evidence." *Entrepreneurship & Regional Development* 29, nos. 1-2, pp. 27-50.

Fixsoftware.com, n.d. "Preventive Maintenance," www.fiixsoftware.com/maintenance-strategies/preventative-maintenance/, (accessed 12 September 2019).

Gallant, M. 2012. "A Simple Definition of Performance Management and Why Everyone Plays a Role." www.saba.com/uk/blog/a-simple-definition-of-performance-managementand-why-everyone-plays-a-role, (accessed 6 August 2019).

Gao, S.S., M.C. Sung, and J. Zhang. 2013. "Risk Management Capability Building in SMEs: A Social Capital Perspective." *International Small Business Journal* 31, no. 6, pp. 677-700.

Gaul, M. 2013. "Five Areas of Human Capital Risk," www.proformascreening.com/blog/2013/08/01/human-capital-infographic/, (accessed 6 September 2019).

Campopiano, G., A. De Massis, and L. Cassia. 2012. "Corporate Social Responsibility: A Survey among SMEs in Bergamo." *Procedia—Social and Behavioral Sciences* 62, pp. 325-41.

Graafland, J. and H. Smid. 2016. "Environmental Impacts of SMEs and the Effects of Formal Management Tools: Evidence from EU's Largest Survey." *Corporate Social Responsibility and Environmental Management* 23, no. 5, pp. 297-307.

Guo-Ciang, W. 2017. "Effects of Socially Responsible Supplier Development and Sustainability-Oriented Innovation on Sustainable Development: Empirical Evidence from SMEs." *Corporate Social Responsibility and Environmental Management* 24, no. 6, pp. 661-75.

Halbesleben, K.L. and C.M. Tolbert. 2014. "Small, Local, and Loyal: How Firm Attributes Affect Workers' Organizational Commitment." *Local Economy: The Journal of the Local Economy Policy Unit* 29, no. 8, pp. 795-809.

Halme, M. and M. Korpela. 2014. "Responsible Innovation Toward Sustainable Development in Small and Medium-Sized Enterprises: A Resource Perspective." *Business Strategy and the Environment* 23, no. 8, pp. 547-66.

Hatak, I., A. Floh, and A. Zauner. 2015. "Working on a Dream: Sustainable Organisational Change in SMEs using the Example of the Austrian Wine Industry." *Review of Managerial Science* 9, no. 2, pp. 285-315.

Henriques, J. and J. Catarino. 2015. "Sustainable Value and Cleaner Production—Research and Application in 19 Portuguese SME." *Journal of Cleaner Production* 96, pp. 379-86.

IISD, n.d. "Sustainable development," www.iisd.org/topic/sustainable-development (accessed 28 September 2019).

Investinganswers.com, n.d. "Gross Domestic Product (GDP)," https://investinganswers.com/dictionary/g/gross-domestic-product-gdp, (accessed 22 September 2019).

Igi–global.com, n.d.a. "What is Cognitive Capital," www.igi-global.com/dictionary/community-production/4200, (accessed 6 September 2019).

Igi–global.com, n.d.b. "What is Structural Capital," www.igi-global.com/dictionary/innovation-in-extremadura/28478, (accessed 6 September 2019).

Igi–global.com, n.d.c. "What is Relational Capital," www.igi-global.com/dictionary/critical-success-factors-core-competencies/24934, (accessed 6 September 2019).

Joernlengsfeld.com, n.d. "Definition Innopreneurship," https://joern-lengsfeld.com/en/definition/innopreneurship/, (accessed 5 September 2019).

Jurevicius, O. 2013. "Resource Based View," www.strategicmanagementinsight.com/topics/resource-based-view.html, (accessed 25 September 2019).

Kajalo, S. and A. Lindblom. 2015. "Market Orientation, Entrepreneurial Orientation and Business Performance among Small Retailers." *International Journal of Retail & Distribution Management* 43, no. 7, pp. 580-96.

Karaoulanis, A. 2017. "Financial Impediments in Risk Management Mechanisms of Greek Small and Medium Enterprises." *International Journal of Management and Information Technology* 12, no. 1, pp. 3128-52.

Karaoulanis, A. 2016. "Ethical Consequences in Business Decision Process." *Journal of Social Sciences Research* 10, no. 4, pp. 2222-8.

Ketprapakorn, N. and S. Kantabutra. 2019. "Culture Development for Sustainable SMEs: Toward a Behavioral Theory." *Sustainability* 11, no. 9, p. 2629.

Keyvani, S.M.A. 2011. "Recent Developments in the Study of Operating and Marketing Strategy Factors in the Formulation of Strategies of

Small Manufacturers." *Journal of Economics and Business Research* 1, pp. 127-35.

Kim, W.C. and R. Mauborgne. 2005. "Blue Ocean Strategy: From Theory to Practice." *California Management Review* 47, no. 3, pp. 105-21.

Kiser, E.K., R.A. Prager, and J.R. Scott. 2016. "Supervisory Ratings and Bank Lending to Small Businesses during the Financial Crisis and Great Recession." *Journal of Financial Services Research* 50, no. 2, pp. 163-86.

Klewitz, J. and E.G. Hansen. 2014. "Sustainability-Oriented Innovation of SMEs: A Systematic Review." *Journal of Cleaner Production* 65, pp. 57-75.

Knowledge-management-tools.net. 2018. "Knowledge Management Definition," www.knowledge-management-tools.net/knowledge-management-definition.html, (accessed 13 September 2019).

Kotey, B. and C. Folker. 2007. "Employee Training in SMEs: Effect of Size and Firm Type-Family and Nonfamily." *Journal of Small Business Management* 45, no. 2, pp. 214-38.

Kraus, S., J.P.C. Rigtering, M. Hughes, and V. Hosman. 2012. "Entrepreneurial Orientation and the Business Performance of SMEs: A Quantitative Study from the Netherlands." *Review of Managerial Science* 6, no. 2, pp. 161-82.

Kęstutis, K. and J. Greblikaitė. 2007. "Entrepreneurship in Sustainable Development: SMEs Innovativeness in Lithuania." *Engineering Economics* 4, no. 54, pp. 20-6.

Krishnan, M.R. and C. Ganesh. 2014. "Implementing Corporate Sustainable Development: A Case of an SME from India." *South Asian Journal of Business and Management Cases* 3, no. 2, pp. 169-77.

Kudlyak, M. and J.M. Sánchez.. 2017. "Revisiting the Behavior of Small and Large Firms during the 2008 Financial Crisis." *Journal of Economic Dynamics and Control* 77, pp. 48-69.

Lai, K.-K., T.-S. Hung, M.-Y. Hsu, and W.T. Lin. 2011. "An Innovative Model of Blue Ocean Strategy and Niche Marketing in Green Industry: A Case Study of the Smart LED Industry." *IEEE,* pp.1-7.

Laurenţiu, R.M. 2016. "Importance of SMEs in European Countries Economy. "*Analele Universităţii Constantin Brâncuşi Din Târgu Jiu: Seria Economie* 1, no. 3, pp. 174-7.

Laurinkevičiūtė, A. and Ž. Stasiškienė. 2011. "SMS for Decision Making of SMEs." *Clean Technologies and Environmental Policy* 13, no. 6, pp. 797-807.

Lepoutre, J. and A. Heene. 2006. "Investigating the Impact of Firm Size on Small Business Social Responsibility: A Critical Review." *Journal of Business Ethics* 67, no. 3, pp. 257-73.

Levine, J. 2018. *Great Mondays: How to Design a Company Culture Employees Love.* 1st ed. New York, NY: McGraw-Hill.

Mäenpää, I. and R. Voutilainen. 2012. "Insurances for Human Capital Risk Management in SMEs." *Vine* 42, no. 1, pp. 52-66.

Malik, K. and A. Jasińska-Biliczak. 2018. "Innovations and Other Processes as Identifiers of Contemporary Trends in the Sustainable Development of SMEs: The Case of Emerging Regional Economies." *Sustainability* 10, no. 5, p. 1361.

Mayr, S., C. Mitter, and A. Aichmayr. 2017. "Corporate Crisis and Sustainable Reorganization: Evidence from Bankrupt Austrian SMEs." *Journal of Small Business Management* 55, no. 1, pp. 108-27.

Mayr, S. and D. Lixl. 2019. "Restructuring in SMEs—A Multiple Case Study Analysis." *Journal of Small Business Strategy* 29, no. 1, pp. 85-98.

Medakovic, V. and S. Vaskovic. 2015. "SMEs in the Function Sustainable Development with Aspect of the use of Renewable Energy." *Acta Technica Corviniensis–Bulletin of Engineering* 8, no. 2, p. 53.

Medforth, T. 2016. "How to Take Advantage of Technology to Improve Your Company Culture." *Strategic HR Review* 15, no. 1, p. 43.

Mills, K.G. and B. McCarthy. 2014. "The State of Small Business Lending: Credit Access During the Recovery and How Technology May Change the Game." Harvard Business School Working Paper, No. 15-004, July 2014.

Moody's. 2016. "Seven Key Challenges in Assessing SME Credit Risk," www.moodysanalytics.com/-/media/whitepaper/2016/seven-key-challenges-assessing%20small-medium-enterprises-sme-credit-risk.pdf, (accessed 6 September 2019).

Myaccountingcourse, n.d.a. "What are Management Control Systems (MCS)?" www.myaccountingcourse.com/accounting-dictionary/management-control-systems, (accessed 11 September 2019).

Myaccountingcourse.com, n.d.b. "What Are Angel Investors?" www .myaccountingcourse.com/accounting-dictionary/angel-investors, (accessed 21 September 2019).

My-e-health.se, n.d. Homepage, www.my-e-health.se/, (accessed 28 September 2019).

Negoescu, G. 2011. "Considerations on the Application of Blue Ocean Strategy to Avoid the Risk of Bankruptcy to Small Enterprises." *Risk in Contemporary Economy* 1, pp. 123-31.

Nlsinfo.org, n.d. "National Longitudinal Surveys," www.nlsinfo.org/content/ getting-started/what-are-longitudinal-data, (accessed 3 Septemeber 2019).

Office of the United States Trade Representative, n.d. "Small- and Medium-Sized Enterprises (SMEs)," https://ustr.gov/trade-agree- ments/free-trade-agreements/transatlantic-trade-and-investment- partnership-t-tip/t-tip-12, (accessed 3 June 2019).

Ogawa, K. and T. Tanaka. 2013. "The Global Financial Crisis and Small- and Medium-Sized Enterprises in Japan: How Did They Cope with the Crisis?" *Small Business Economics* 41, no. 2, pp. 401-17.

Olmos-Peñuela, J., A. García-Granero, E. Castro-Martínez, and P. D'Este. 2017. "Strengthening SMEs' Innovation Culture through Collaborations with Public Research Organizations: Do All Firms Benefit Equally?" *European Planning Studies* 25, no. 11, pp. 2001-20.

Quaye, D. and I. Mensah. 2019. "Marketing Innovation and Sustainable Competitive Advantage of Manufacturing SMEs in Ghana." *Manage- ment Decision* 57, no. 7, pp. 1535-53.

Papazov, E. and L. Mihaylova. 2016. "Using Key 'Blue Ocean' Tools for Strategy Rethinking of a SME: A Case from the Bulgarian Knitwear Industry." *Economics and Business* 29, no. 1, pp. 104-10.

Papke, Edgar and Inc. Books24x7. 2013. *True Alignment: Linking Com- pany Culture with Customer Needs for Extraordinary Results.* US: Amacom.

Peric, M. and V. Vitezic. 2016. "Impact of Global Economic Crisis on Firm Growth." *Small Business Economics* 46, no. 1, pp. 1-12.

Research Institute of Economy, Trade and Industry (RIETI), n.d. "What is RIETI," www.rieti.go.jp/en/, (accessed 20 June 2019).

Roxas, B. and D. Chadee. 2016. "Knowledge Management View of Environmental Sustainability in Manufacturing SMEs in the Philippines." *Knowledge Management Research & Practice* 14, no. 4, pp. 514-24.

Sääskilahti, J. 2016. "Local Bank Competition and Small Business Lending After the Onset of the Financial Crisis." *Journal of Banking and Finance* 69, pp. 37-51.

Sahut, J. and M. Peris-Ortiz. 2014. "Small Business, Innovation, and Entrepreneurship." *Small Business Economics* 42, no. 4, pp.663-8.

Salimzadeh, P. and J. Courvisanos. 2015. "A Conceptual Framework for Assessing Sustainable Development in Regional SMEs." *Journal of Environmental Assessment Policy and Management* 17, no. 4, pp. 1-17.

Sciencedirect.com, n.d. "Logit Model," www.sciencedirect.com/topics/economics-econometrics-and-finance/logit-model, (accessed 3 September 2019).

Shiraishi, G.F. and S. Barbosa. 2015. *Strategy Formulation and Organizational Structure in SMEs: Taking Business Models Beyond the Hands of the Founders*, pp. 658-69.

Sime, C. 2019. "The Cost of Ignoring Mental Health in the Workplace," www.forbes.com/sites/carleysime/2019/04/17/the-cost-of-ignoring-mental-health-in-the-workplace/#5a8df3b53726, (accessed 28 September 2019).

Smulders, S. and G. Naidoo. 2013. "Addressing the Small Business Tax Compliance Burden: Evidence from South Africa." *Journal of Economic and Financial Sciences* 6, no. 1, pp. 33-54.

Sopheon.com, n.d. "Sustainable Product Development," www.sopheon.com/sustainable-product-development/, (accessed 11 September 2019).

Soriano, D.R. and J.M.C. Martínez. 2007. "Transmitting the Entrepreneurial Spirit to the Work Team in SMEs: The Importance of Leadership." *Management Decision* 45, no. 7, pp. 1102-22.

Spithoven, A., W. Vanhaverbeke, and N. Roijakkers. 2013. "Open Innovation Practices in SMEs and Large Enterprises." *Small Business Economics* 41, no. 3, pp. 537-62.

Stoian, C. and M. Gilman. 2017. "Corporate Social Responsibility that "Pays": A Strategic Approach to CSR for SMEs." *Journal of Small Business Management* 55, no. 1, pp. 5-31.

Study.com, n.d. "Turnaround Management: Definition and Process," https://study.com/academy/lesson/turnaround-management-definition-process.html, (accessed 28 September 2019).

Sudek, Richard. 2006. "Angel Investment Criteria." *Journal of Small Business Strategy* 17, no. 2, p. 89.

Sungjoo, L., G. Park, J. Park, and B. Yoon. 2010. "Open Innovation in SMEs—An Intermediated Network Model." *Research Policy* 39, no. 2, pp. 290-300.

Susomrith, P. and A. Coetzer. 2015. "Employees' Perceptions of Barriers to Participation in Training and Development in Small Engineering Businesses." *Journal of Workplace Learning* 27, no. 7, pp. 561-78.

Swistak, A. 2016. "Tax Penalties in SME Tax Compliance." *Financial Theory and Practice* 40, no. 1, pp. 129-47.

Systemdynamics.org, n.d. "What is System Dynamics," www.systemdynamics.org/what-is-sd, (accessed 6 August 2019).

Szczepańska-Woszczyna, K. and J. Kurowska-Pysz. 2016. "Sustainable Business Development through Leadership in SMEs." *Ekonomia i Zarzadzanie* 8, no. 3, pp. 57-69.

The World Bank, n.d. "Small and Medium Enterprises (SMEs) Finance," www.worldbank.org/en/topic/smefinance, (accessed 3 June 2019).

Thurik, R. and S. Wennekers. 2004. "Entrepreneurship, Small Business and Economic Growth." *Journal of Small Business and Enterprise Development* 11, no. 1, pp. 140-9.

Tokognon, J.P.R. and S. Yunfei. 2018. "Innovation Policy for Sustainable Development of SMEs in Benin." *IEEE.* doi:10.1109/GTSD.2018.8595524.

Tsai, W.-H. and W.-C. Chou. 2009. "Selecting Management Systems for Sustainable Development in SMEs: A Novel Hybrid Model Based on DEMATEL, ANP, and ZOGP." *Expert Systems with Applications* 36, no. 2, pp. 1444-58.

Tse, T. and K. Soufani. 2003. "Business Strategies for Small Firms in the New Economy." *Journal of Small Business and Enterprise Development* 10, no. 3, pp. 306-20.

Verreynne, M.-L. and D. Meyer. 2010. "Small Business Strategy and the Industry Life Cycle." *Small Business Economics* 35, no. 4, pp. 399-416.

Wagener, S., M. Gorgievski, and S. Rijsdijk. 2010. "Businessman or Host? Individual Differences between Entrepreneurs and Small Business Owners in the Hospitality Industry." *The Service Industries Journal* 30, no. 9, pp. 1513-27.

Ward, S. 2019. "What is a Venture Capitalist," www.thebalancesmb.com/what-is-a-venture-capitalist-2947071, (accessed 21 September 2019).

Wiebke, B. and A. Winkler. 2016. "Flexible or Fragile? The Growth Performance of Small and Young Businesses during the Global Financial Crisis—Evidence from Germany." *Journal of Business Venturing* 31, no. 2, pp. 196-215.

Wiklund, J. and D. Shepherd. 2003. "Knowledge-Based Resources, Entrepreneurial Orientation, and the Performance of Small and Medium-Sized Businesses." *Strategic Management Journal* 24, no. 13, pp. 1307-14.

Wiklund, J., D. Shepherd, JIBS Entrepreneurship Centre, IHH, Centre for Innovation Systems, Entrepreneurship and Growth, Högskolan i Jönköping, IHH, EMM (Entreprenörskap, Marknadsföring, Management), and Internationella Handelshögskolan. 2005. "Entrepreneurial Orientation and Small Business Performance: A Configurational Approach." *Journal of Business Venturing* 20, no. 1, pp. 71-91.

Woodward, L. and L.M. Tan. 2015. "Small Business Owners' Attitudes Toward GST Compliance: A Preliminary Study." *Australian Tax Forum* 30, no. 3, pp. 517-49.

Žigienė, G., E. Rybakovas, and R. Alzbutas. 2019. "Artificial Intelligence Based Commercial Risk Management Framework for SMEs." *Sustainability* 11, no. 16, p. 4501.

About the Author

Andreas Karaoulanis, MBA, MSc, Eng., MSc B.Eng, is an academic and a business persona. He holds a masters in engineering from Aristotle University of Thessaloniki, Greece; an MBA in industrial management and economics from Blekinge Institute of Technology, Sweden, with distinction; a masters in decision support and risk analysis from Stockholm University, Sweden, with high distinction; and he is about to complete his masters in information systems from Linnaeus University. He is the author of *Paragons Involved in Strategy Implementation. A Holistic Approach*, *Risk Management and Decision Making in Strategy Implementation*, and *Distance Learning: Paragons Involved and Social Implications*.

He has published many papers in different international peer-reviewed scientific journals; he is a peer reviewer of several other journals in two continents. His papers are read via academia.edu in more than 135 countries, as we speak. He has international research experience as he has conducted researches with U.S, Asian, and European universities on business and tourism.

He is a growth expert and a strategist in many industries as his unique approach to business is extremely successful in many different industries where it has been used till now. He has been in top managerial and C-suite positions since the last 25 years in several industries such as banking, automotive, apparel and fashion, retail, digital marketing, academia, consulting, insurance, engineering, startups, and as an author, while he is an active seminar lecturer on business topics. He is also a business coach, a blogger, and a LinkedIn influencer with many thousands of followers.

Index

OTHER TITLES IN THE ENTREPRENEURSHIP AND SMALL BUSINESS MANAGEMENT COLLECTION

Scott Shane, Case Western University, *Editor*

- *Startup Strategy Humor: Democratizing Startup Strategy* by Rajesh K. Pillania
- *The Leadership Development Journey: How Entrepreneurs Develop Leadership Through Their Lifetime* by Jen Vuhuong
- *Getting to Market With Your MVP: How to Achieve Small Business and Entrepreneur Success* by J.C. Baker
- *Can You Run Your Business With Blood, Sweat, and Tears? Volume I: Blood* by Stephen Elkins-Jarrett and Nick Skinner
- *Can You Run Your Business With Blood, Sweat, and Tears? Volume II: Sweat* by Stephen Elkins-Jarrett and Nick Skinner
- *Can You Run Your Business With Blood, Sweat, and Tears? Volume III: Tear* by Stephen Elkins-Jarrett and Nick Skinner
- *Family Business Governance: Increasing Business Effectiveness and Professionalism* by Keanon J. Alderson
- *Department of Startup: Why Every Fortune 500 Should Have One* by Ivan Yong Wei Kit and Sam Lee
- *The Rainmaker: Start-Up to Conglomerate* by Jacques Magliolo
- *Get on Board: Earning Your Ticket to a Corporate Board Seat* by Olga V. Mack
- *From Vision to Decision: A Self-Coaching Guide to Starting a New Business* by Dana K. Dwyer
- *Cultivating an Entrepreneurial Mindset* by Tamiko L. Cuellar
- *On All Cylinders, Second Edition: Succeeding as an Entrepreneur and a Leader* by Ron Robinson
- *The Entrepreneurial Adventure: Embracing Risk, Change, and Uncertainty* by David James and Oliver James

Announcing the Business Expert Press Digital Library

Concise e-books business students need for classroom and research

This book can also be purchased in an e-book collection by your library as

- a one-time purchase,
- that is owned forever,
- allows for simultaneous readers,
- has no restrictions on printing, and
- can be downloaded as PDFs from within the library community.

Our digital library collections are a great solution to beat the rising cost of textbooks. E-books can be loaded into their course management systems or onto students' e-book readers.

The **Business Expert Press** digital libraries are very affordable, with no obligation to buy in future years. For more information, please visit **www.businessexpertpress.com/librarians**. To set up a trial in the United States, please email **sales@businessexpertpress.com**.

CPSIA information can be obtained
at www.ICGtesting.com
Printed in the USA
JSHW020825190520
5759JS00006B/143